LINGUOPOETICS OF THE WORKS OF MURAD MUHAMMAD DOST

ABDUMALIK HAMIDOV

© Taemeer Publications LLC
Linguopoetics of the works of Murad Muhammad Dost
by: Abdumalik Hamidov
Edition: August '2023
Publisher:
Taemeer Publications LLC (Michigan, USA / Hyderabad, India)

ISBN 978-93-5872-131-7

© Taemeer Publications

Book	:	Linguopoetics of the works of Murad Muhammad Dost
Author	:	Abdumalik Hamidov
Publisher	:	Taemeer Publications
Year	:	'2023
Pages	:	192
Title Design	:	*Taemeer Web Design*

Tashkent - 2021

The issue of the use of artistic text and language materials in it is one of the main issues related to the artist's ability to use words. Accordingly, studying and analyzing the appropriate use of language tools in an artistic work is one of the general philological problems.

The monograph analyzes the textual structure of Murad Muhammad Dost's works, language features, the writer's ability to use vocabulary tools to create characters' characters.

Responsible Editor:
Umurkulov Bekpo'lat,
doctor of philological sciences

Reviewers:
Yakub Saidov,
doctor of philological sciences, professor.
Mukhtarali Zakirov,
doctor of philological sciences, professor.

INTRODUCTION

Since the second half of the 20th century, the scope of research interpreting the language of artistic works and the poetic function of words in artistic texts has been expanding. As a result of such researches, it becomes possible to determine the function of national language tools based on their realization in speech processes and to determine the factors that show the aesthetic effectiveness of language tools.

From the second half of the last century, by examining the fiction literature of each nation, a large place was devoted to the research of the language of fiction aimed at solving such urgent issues as researching the incomparable spiritual wealth of this nation, determining the ability of the creator to use the language, the extraordinary character of the speech construction of the writer's works, the uniqueness of expression. As a result of such research, new methods of studying the use of language in artistic texts are created, linguistics is enriched with various theoretical conclusions. The scientific significance of studying artistic speech, the text of works of a creator from the point of view of the artistic-aesthetic function of language means is that the place of language means in the speech process is evaluated, and the relationship between language and speech is theoretically based.

Uzbek linguistics in the years of independence significant progress has been made in the interpretation of fiction as a creative-individual style, in the analysis of the figurative-impressiveness of artistic speech, which shows the artistic-aesthetic value. As a result, studies based on linguopoetic interpretation, which show the possibilities of using linguistic tools for the purpose, and show the individuality in the use of words, have come to the field. In current Uzbek linguopoetics, there is an increasing need to analyze the artistic work, to use various research methods of world linguistics to illuminate the poetic skills of the creator, as well as to thoroughly research issues such as creative individuality and literary influence in creating an artistic image, comparative-typological, generality and uniqueness with examples of world literature . "Literature shows the heart of the people, the spirituality of the people. In today's complex times, it is necessary to use the impressive power of literature to find a way to people's hearts and inspire them to noble goals [1]. Unveiling the impressive power of literature is one of the important tasks of linguopoetics.

---

[1]The speech of the President of the Republic of Uzbekistan Shavkat Mirziyoyev during his visit to the "Alley of Writers" // Xalq sozi, 2020, May 21. #106 (7608)

FUNDAMENTALS OF ARTISTIC TEXT EXPRESSION AND LINGUISTIC POSSIBILITIES

Linguistic study of literary text in Uzbek linguistics

Since the linguistic analysis of the literary text is one of the important issues of linguistics, the scope of research in this direction is expanding year by year. It is known that an artistic text is a unique form of expression, any artistic expression is a mirror reflecting human life and worldview. That is why the artistic text is a criterion that expresses, determines and evaluates the human lifestyle. Accordingly, the artistic text is macro and micro-texts that reflect the national language in fiction, and show artistic-imagery, aesthetically impressive appearance. For this reason, the study of the language of fiction is of both theoretical and practical importance for the science of linguistics and remains one of the topical issues.

The language of fiction differs sharply from other forms of language in terms of task. Therefore, the language of fiction requires both linguistic and aesthetic analysis according to its general basis.

In the years of independence, a new period of linguistic study of artistic text in Uzbek linguistics began. After the independence of our country, the study of national history, literature, and language on a large scale is being given special importance. In scientific research, attention has been paid to the study of the language of the artistic work, the language and style of the writer, to the analysis of all aspects of the linguistic means in artistic texts. New methods of literary text analysis have appeared. It is known that in Uzbek linguistics, the study of the language of artistic works began in the 50s of the 20th century. During this period, the opinions of scholars such as Sh.Shoabdurahmonov, A.Gulomov, I.Sultan, G'.Abdurahmonov, Kh.Doniyorov, Q.Samadov, N.Shukurov were expressed in the articles about the skill of using artistic language. Later, in the 80s and 90s, a number of works were published that researched the language skills of many writers, the language and style of a work. The scientific works of researchers such as B.Yoldoshev, B.Yoryev, S.Karimov, B.Umurqulov, M.Yoldoshev, R.Normurodov, S.Boymirzaeva, G.Muhammadjonova on the study of works of art served for the further development of this research direction [2]. Undoubtedly, this type of research had a great impact on the development of language research, in particular, new methods of studying the

---

[2]Yuldoshev B. Yazyk i stil produced by Saida Akhma. Autoref. diss. ... candy. Philol. science -Tashkent, 1979; Karimov S. Yazyk i st il proizvedeniy Zulfii. Autoref. diss.... cand. Philol. science - T a shkent , 1982; Yariev B. Language poetry Maksuda Sheikhzade. Autoref. diss.... cand. Philol. science - T a shkent , 1979; Umurkulov B. Leksicheskie osobennosti sovremennoy Uzbekskoy poeticheskoy rechi. d iss.... sugar Philol. science - T a shkent , 1993; Yoldoshev M. Cholpon's artistic language skills. Philol. science. name ...diss.. autoref. - Tashkent, 2000; Normurodov R. Language features of Shukur Kholmirzaev's works. Philol. science. name ... diss. autoref. - Tashkent, 2000; Boymirzaeva S. A linguistic study of Oybek's prose. Philol. science. name ... diss. autoref. - Samarkand, 2004. Muhammadjonova G. Lingupoetic study of Uzbek poetry of the late 80s and early 90s. Philol. science. name ... diss. autoref. - Tashkent, 2004.

use of language in artistic texts were created, language materials used in artistic texts, the language and style of the works of talented writers began to be widely studied. However, the lexical and stylistic features of the work of a number of leading writers of Uzbek literature have not been linguistically studied by linguists as an object of special research.

Academician G. Abdurakhmanov noted that the artistic skill and unique style of a writer or poet can be revealed by analyzing the language of an artistic work. Therefore, it should be one of the main issues to study the language of each artistic work in depth and from all sides [3]. Because the work of art appears as an example of human thinking, understanding and description of the world. This process cannot be imagined without language. Language materials form the basis of any creative activity. Each artist's style of using language, skill in using language tools in speech is unique. This, in turn, creates individuality. For this reason, G. Abdurahmanov emphasized the importance of learning the language of each artistic work. Analyzing the language of a work of art, studying the language features of each creator's works, revealing the richness of the national language, and determining the creator's contribution to the development of a particular language are important. It is also seen that it is one of the urgent problems of studying and

---

[3] Abdurakhmanov G'. About learning the language of a literary work // Issues of the methodology of teaching the Uzbek language. -Tashkent, 1966. -B. 7.

analyzing the language of fiction, that the language of fiction is of deep importance in determining the ways of literary language development.

It is known that the language of Uzbek fiction is studied mainly in the linguistic and stylistic aspect, and in recent years the methods of researching the language of artistic works are expanding. This provides an opportunity to more widely illuminate the function of language tools in artistic texts. Because the language tools do not remain a means of expressing ideas and concepts in an artistic work, but serve the imagery that forms the basis of an artistic work and ensure that it fulfills an aesthetic function. Accordingly, the language of fiction is a figurative language that performs both communicative and aesthetic functions. This case shows the breadth of the functional range of the language of fiction. One of the factors determining the specific characteristics of the language of literary literature is the expressiveness of the language of the artistic work. Its basis is the skillful use of language tools. Accordingly, the writer's effective use of language capabilities is evaluated as his skill. The writer's ability to use words, appropriate use of words in the process of artistic expression is an important artistic quality that determines the artistic value of the work.

Every element of language skillfully used in a work of art is an important resource in describing events, revealing characters, and serves to ensure the expressiveness and imagery of the artistic text. For this reason, creators try to enrich the language of their works with unique allusions and images by effectively using the possibilities of the universal language. In this process, on the basis of artistic texts, the national language is refined, and the available possibilities of language tools are clarified. The choice of normative means of the literary language, its polishing, serves the enrichment of the literary language. This situation requires a special study of the language of fiction.

As mentioned above, the study of the language of fiction in Uzbek linguistics began in the 60s of the 20th century [4], and mainly the linguistic features of poetic works were analyzed. It is worth noting that in Uzbek linguistics, the coverage of this topic was carried out mostly on the basis of poetic speech materials, and the study of the use of language tools in the prose text became much stronger in the years of independence. Prof. one of the first researchers of artistic prose language. It was I. Kochkortoev. The scientist was one of the first in Uzbek

---

Kuchkartaev I. Phraseological innovation of A. Kahkhara. Abstract diss.... cand. philol. Sciences. - Tashkent, 1965; Samadov K. Some questions of Aibek's language skills. Abstract diss. ... cand. philol. Sciences. – Tashkent, 1967; Nasirov U. The language and style of the novel "Sisters" by Askad Mukhtor. Abstract diss. ... cand. philol. Sciences. - Samarkand, 1968; Kilichev E. Archaisms and historicisms in the prose of Sadriddin Aina. Abstract Diss. ...cand. philol. Sciences. – Tashkent, 1969

linguistics to analyze the phraseological features of the language of A. Qahhor's works.

Another of the first studies analyzed in connection with the writer's skill of using words in the language of artistic works is Q. Samadov's candidate's thesis on the study of the language of Oibek works.

In this work, the researcher analyzed the language skills of the writer, how he selected and sorted out language tools in his works to show that the vernacular is an inexhaustible treasure. As it is known, Oibek's works reflect the periods characteristic of our nation's past, so the researcher attached special importance to defining his skill in using historical and archaic words in his works. In this way, the researcher pays special attention to the reflection of the spirit of the time in words.

The researcher found out that Oybek is a clever connoisseur of the treasure of the folk language, his skill in using words, skillfully using synonyms, figurative words, repeated words, as well as words specific to the folk colloquial speech.

In this first study of the artistic prose language of Q. Samadov, the writer's art of using words, the fact that the used words ensure the naturalness of the speech of the characters and the truthfulness of the image, that they are the specific words of the period, therefore they serve as vocabulary tools that increase the value of the artistic work, reveal the image of the heroes , which analyzed on the basis of examples that Oybek's skill in using words is high. This large-scale research work was the impetus for the creation of many dissertations.

B. Yoldoshev's dissertation devoted to the analysis of the language and style of Said Ahmed's works is one of such studies [5].

After these studies, there were no works devoted to the analysis of artistic prose language in Uzbek linguistics for many years. In the years of independence, the study of the language of literary literature, especially the language of literary prose, became stronger. A number of dissertations and monographs have been published in this field [6].

---

[5]Yuldashev B. Yazyk i stil produced by Saida Akhma. Autoref. diss.... sugar Philol. science -Tashkent, 1979.
[6]Karimov S. Artistic style of the Uzbek language. - Samarkand, 1992; Umurkulov B. Word in fiction. -Tashkent, 1993; Karimov S. Artistic style of the Uzbek language. Philol. Doctor of Sciences diss. ... autoref. - Tashkent, 1993; Yoldoshev M. Cholpon's artistic language skills. Philol. science. name ... diss. autoref. -Tashkent, 2000; Normurodov R. Language features of Shukur Kholmirzaev's works. Philol. science. name ... diss. autoref. - Tashkent, 2000; Boymirzaeva S. A linguistic study of Oybek's prose. Philol. science. name ... diss. autoref. - Samarkand, 2004; Jalolova L. Linguistic study of Abdulla Qadiri's novel "O'tkan kunlar". Philol. science. name ... diss. autoref. - Tashkent, 2007; Kasimova M. Linguistic features of the individuality of artistic speech (on the example of Togay Murad's works) Filol. science. name ... diss. autoref. - Tashkent, 2007; Hasanov A. Lexical-stylistic tools that ensure the artistic language of Abdulla Qahhor's stories. Philol. science. name ... diss. autoref. - Tashkent, 2010; Yoldoshev M. Secrets of the word shepherd. -Tashkent, 2002; Normurodov R. Artistic skills of Shukur Kholmirzaev. - Tashkent: Literary Fund of the Writers' Union of Uzbekistan, 2003. -103.

Prof. S. Karimov's monograph "Artistic style of the Uzbek language" is one of the first studies in the linguistic research of artistic style. In the work, the place of artistic style within the framework of functional styles, the tools that create artistic style, and the study of artistic style are analyzed. The researcher thinks about the artistic style: "Another important aspect necessary for us to fully imagine the artistic style is the question of the personality of the writer in its formation. "Writer's work on words means that he repeatedly examines the text in the process of creation, works to make the plot, image, image and narrative effective," he writes. It seems that one of the important tools that creates an artistic style is the writer's work on words, skillful use of language tools.

The researcher stated that, due to the individual style of the writer in connection with the genre characteristics of the artistic work, the artistic text goes out of the scope of the literary language, as a result of which all the glosses of the richness of the national language are reflected in the literary literature [7]. Such freedom and universality in the use of language tools shows that the artistic text has its own way of expression. This situation indicates that studying the language of an artistic work, analyzing it, and coming to conclusions are among the problems of linguistics.

---

[7]Karimov S. Featured work. - B. 36.

The researcher singled out phonetic, grammatical and lexical tools as factors in the creation of artistic style and analyzed their characteristics in creating artistic style. In particular, when thinking about the lexical features of an artistic text, special attention is paid to the fact that the word has connotative, emotional-expressive meanings, is specific for a certain speech, and also has the features of signifying different relations of the speaker. Because art is an important part of an artistic work, words become a means of enhancing art with these characteristics.

Another of the researches, where the important features of the literary text are expressed, is the monograph of B. Umurkulov entitled "Word in Literary Literature" [8]. The research discusses the specific features of artistic prose. The issues related to the literary language and literary norm of the prose speech are explained, common words, bookish words, words specific to oral speech, figurative tools are analyzed as the main vocabulary tools of artistic prose. After these studies, a number of other works devoted to the study of the language of artistic prose were created. One of such researches is M. Yoldoshev's monograph "The Secrets of the Cholpon Word" [9].

While thinking about the role of Cholpon in the development of the Uzbek literary language, the researcher

---

[8] Umurkulov B. Word in fiction. - Tashkent, 1993.
[9] Yoldoshev M. Secrets of the word shepherd. - Tashkent, 2002.

shows the aesthetic essence of the Uzbek language based on the use of synonyms, antonyms, polysemous words, obsolete words, slang words, foreign and rude words, expressions, proverbs and proverbs. and also reveals the artistic image of the work based on the use of pictorial means. As you know, words with meaning are the wealth of language and all creative people use these tools. However, the use of synonyms has its own advantages. Therefore, the researcher finds it necessary to pay attention to two aspects of Cholpon's ability to use meaningful words: "One of them is the writer's choice of two or more meaningful words for the content to be expressed, and the second is the harmonious combination of two or more meaningful units in one text for the purpose of artistic image. he specifically emphasizes that "use" [10].

As a characteristic of the writer's style in the use of synonyms, the researcher finds that one of the synonyms has an excess of symbols, master, skillful, skillful; he showed on the basis of the usage of the synonyms of factor, mirishkor, farang. It is also analyzed on the basis of examples of the writer's use of meaningful words in strengthening the negative sign, avoiding word repetition, increasing the effectiveness of the expression, and detailing the described event.

---

[10] Yoldoshev M. Featured work. - B. 11.

It is known that pictorial means make up an important part of artistic imagery in a work of art. Therefore, in works dedicated to the study of the language of artistic works, visual means are definitely analyzed. In this study, the skill of using pictorial means to ensure the artistic imagery of Cholpon's works is revealed based on the use of simile, metaphor, and animation tools.

Particular importance is attached to the characteristic of the author's individual style of pictorial means, and it is appropriate to separate those belonging to the private author.

The researcher explained the role of Cholpon in the development of Uzbek fiction based on the language tools used in the novel "Night and Kunduz" and their skillful use in accordance with the content of the speech.

Another of the researches devoted to the language characteristics of artistic works is the monograph of R. Normurodov entitled "Artistic skill of Shukur Kholmirzaev" [11].

In the monograph, the writer's works are linguistically analyzed. At first, the lexical composition of the language of the writer's works was discussed, the expression of the word in Sh. Kholmirzaev's works was analyzed based on the writer's ability to use the words in their place, and the language of the work

---

[11]Normurodov R. Language features of Shukur Kholmirzaev's works. Philol. science. name ... diss. autoref. -Tashkent, 2000; Normurodov R. Artistic skills of Shukur Kholmirzaev. - Tashkent: Literary Fund of the Writers' Union of Uzbekistan, 2003. -103.

was refined. Also, in this study, lexical units are classified stylistically, in which the writer's ability to use synonyms and ambiguous words is discussed. In this study, special attention is paid to the analysis of the writer's ability to use visual means.

The writer's skillful use of figurative tools such as periphrasis, simile, metaphor, epithet to enhance artistry and imagery is shown on the basis of examples.

The work pays special attention to the writer's use of non-literary language units. As non-literary units, the issues of the writer's artistry in using dialectisms, oral speech tools, as well as the creation of an occasional word and the ability to absorb it in accordance with the spirit of the text are also deeply analyzed.

In the study "Linguistic features of Uncle Murad's works" by M. Kasimova, the skill of the writer was analyzed based on the use of different level units of the language in the creative process. In particular, the skill of creating an artistic speech is revealed based on the use of phonetic and lexical tools of the writing language, occasional words, anthroponyms (personal names), morphological and syntactic tools, which are important forms of lexical tools. In this dissertation, unlike other studies, the stable compounds used by the writer (proverb, proverb, idioms) are studied separately and the writer's skill in using these tools is evaluated.

In this study, like many other scientific works, the aspects of artistic image tools that create speech individuality are analyzed separately. Metaphor, symbol, irony, and repetition of artistic image tools are analyzed on the example of Togay Murad's works.

In the work, Togay Murad's ability to use dialectisms was studied on the example of phonetic dialectisms, morphological dialectisms, as well as dialectisms that arise on the basis of sound changes, and it was recognized that dialectisms are one of the main tools that ensure the uniqueness of the writer's works, and it was noted that the writer achieved artistic appeal by using dialect elements [12].

Researches devoted to the linguistic analysis of literary prose, as indicated above, were mainly carried out within the linguistic features of the works of one writer. This situation also required the need to conduct many studies in this direction, for example, to conduct research in the field of studying the language characteristics of individual works, the language of works specific to certain genres. As one of such studies, it is possible to show the study of the language of stories by the linguist A. Hasanov [13].

---

[12] Kasimova M. Linguistic characteristics of the individuality of artistic speech (based on the works of Uncle Murad): Filol.fan.nomz. ... diss. autoref. - Tashkent, 2004. -B.14.
[13] Hasanov A. Lexical-stylistic tools that ensure the artistic language of Abdulla Qahhor's stories: Filol.fan.nomz. ... diss. autoref. - Tashkent, 2010.

The research focuses on the figurative use of the word as a means of providing the artistry of the language of stories, as well as the linguopoetic possibilities of such use, the writer's skill in using metaphors, metonymy, and synecdoche. In this study, the use of limited lexicon, units of the non-literary layer, as well as semantic-stylistic units as a means of enhancing the art of narrative language was analyzed. The difference of this research work from other works in this direction is that the method of linguopoetic analysis took the lead in the work, and the enhancement of the artistic and aesthetic effectiveness of the work was revealed through the writer's individual skill in using words.

In Uzbek linguistics, the study of the language of artistic works is mainly devoted to the analysis of the language features of the works of a writer or a poet, and there are not enough studies that reflect the general characteristics of the artistic language and artistic text and encourage the expansion of the scope of the study of the language of artistic works through research in this context. Because of this need, M. Yoldoshev's doctoral dissertation entitled "Linguopoetic study of literary text" was created [14]. This research is aimed at the analysis of the artistic text on a general theoretical basis, in which the essence of the text, the definition of the text, the units that make up the

---

[14]Yoldoshev M. Lingupoetic study of the literary text: Philol. science. doc. ... diss. autoref. - Tashkent, 2009.

text are discussed, and opinions are expressed within the definition of text types.

In the work, the need to approach the analysis of the artistic text from the linguopoetic point of view is emphasized, the meaningful types of the artistic text are defined, the issues of meaning and content in the artistic text are analyzed, and the principles of the linguopoetic analysis of the artistic text are determined. In the researcher's monograph "Linguopoetics of a literary text" [15] the linguopoetic features of the literary text are explained in more detail on the basis of examples. Undoubtedly, this type of research serves as a basis, a source for a large-scale study of the language of artistic texts.

The aspects of the artistic speech related to the word were also analyzed as important issues of Uzbek literary studies [16]. In particular, Y. Solijonov emphasizes that one of the important features of artistic prose is the appropriate use of words in the speech process. He said that the sentence " *Shorahim Shavvaz's wife Aysuluv has been very ill for several*

---

[15] Yoldoshev M. Linguistics of literary text. - Tashkent, 2008.
[16] Toraev D. Problems of artistic thinking and skills in contemporary Uzbek novels (60-80s). Ph.D. ... diss. autoref. - Tashkent, 1994; Solijonov Y. Poetics of artistic speech in Uzbek prose of the 80s-90s of the 20th century: Filol. science. dr. ... diss. autoref. - Tashkent, 2002; Solijonov Y. Speech and style. - Tashkent, 2002; Kuronov D. Poetics of shepherd's prose. - Tashkent, 2004; Kuronov D. Theoretical notes. - Tashkent, 2018; Toraev D. Time and creative responsibility. - Tashkent, 2004; Imamova G. Nationalism and artistic speech. - Tashkent, 2004; Sabirdinov A. Word and image in Oybek's poetry. - Tashkent, 2010.

months " in O. Yakubov's work "Swans, white birds" can be expressed in the form of " Aysuluv has been ill for several months ", but it remains simple information, that is, the essence of the idea that the writer wants to convey is not revealed. , very aptly explained that it will become a general description [17]. D. Kuronov imagines an artistic work as a GAP, and emphasizes that the content of a sentence is related to a number of aspects such as the words that make up it and their grammatical relations, the speaker's personality, his current state of mind, his relationship with the interlocutors, other statements in the conversation process [18]. By this, the scientist refers to the work of art as a type of communication, communication based on artistry and imagery, and its basis is language tools. The scientist looks at the word as a "material of literature" and shows that the word appears in the mind of a person as an image of a thing-phenomenon based on the meaning of reality, the word returns to its original - figurative nature in the artistic speech, and the eternal characteristic of the word is manifested in the artistic speech [19]. Literary scholar G.Imomova, who interpreted artistic speech as a means of individualization, emphasizes that the language of an artistic work requires conformity of form and content, follows the laws of

---

[17] Solijonov Y. Speech and style. - Tashkent, 2002. - B. 15.
[18] Kuronov D. Poetics of shepherd's prose. - Tashkent, 2004. - B. 84.
[19] Kuronov D. Theoretical notes. - Tashkent, 2018. - B. 64.

individualization, and also covers all forms of literary language and lively conversational language with its artistic aesthetic quality [20].

It is known that the artistic speech is formed on the basis of the tools of the national language, therefore, it reflects all the tools of the national language. If these tools are used in artistic speech based on the essence of speech, it becomes a tool of artistic speech. After all, an artistic work is first of all determined by its effectiveness, and effectiveness is created on the basis of appropriate use of language tools. The place of the word as an important tool of the artistic text in creating an image is expressed in the monograph "Word and image in the poetry of Oybek" by literary critic A. Sabirdinov. The scientist says that the skill and talent of every creator is determined by his ability to use the ideological and artistic connotations of the word [21]. In the monograph, the writer analyzed Oybek's ability to use words in creating portraits, landscapes, poetic details, and images. This research work is also noteworthy in terms of reflecting the importance of language tools, which show the important feature of artistic speech, which shows the skill of using words of the writer.

In recent years, linguopoetics as a separate field of linguistics has become an important direction that studies the

---

[20]Imamova G. Nationalism and artistic speech. - Tashkent, 2004. - B. 28.
[21]Sobirdinov A. Word and image in Oybek's poetry. - Tashkent, 2010. - B. 7.

language of artistic works. V. P. Grigorev is a scientist who is specially engaged in the research of theoretical issues of linguopoetics in Russian linguistics [22]. According to him, the subject of linguopoetics is creativity in the manifestation of language. The main object is the language of fiction. Accordingly, he interprets linguopoetics as a philological field that studies the poetics of language [23]. Also, linguopoetics is a teaching that studies the aesthetic function of language in all areas [24]. So, linguopoetics is a field of linguistics that studies the aesthetic properties of language tools. The object of his study is artistic language, that is, a language that has an aesthetic effect on a person based on the expression of thoughts in artistic paints.

Prof. Lingupoetic analysis of artistic text in Uzbek linguistics. It started with N. Mahmudov's articles on the interpretation of this topic [25]. In these articles, very important ideas about the linguopoetics of the artistic text were put forward. In the article "Linguopoetics of similes in Oybek's poetry", which discusses the linguopoetic features of the figurative tool of simile, the scientist puts forward the opinion that the artistic value of simile depends on the standard of

---

[22] Grigorev V.P. Poetics is a word. - M., 1979;
[23] Grigorev V.P. Poetics and words. - p. 58.
[24] Grigorev V.P. Poetics and words. - p. 59.
[25] Mahmudov N. Linguistics of similes in Oybek's poetry // Uzbek language and literature. - Tashkent, 1985. - #6. - B. 48-50.

simile. In fact, the originality and novelty of the standard of simile is the most important aspect of this visual tool, and the provision of artistic imagery in the text depends on the novelty of the standard of simile. The linguopoetics of the text emerges as a result of the content and grammatical connection of each word used in the text with other words. Therefore, when N. Mahmudov thinks about the linguopoetics of similes, the coincidence of the simile subject and standard gives special importance to the contrast between the simile subject and the simile standard [26]. This kind of contrast leads to an increase in the aesthetic value, pictoriality, and imagery of the simile.

In the interpretation of the linguopoetic possibilities of the word, it should be recognized that the scientist's work devoted to the linguopoetic study of Abdulla Qahhor's stories served as a very important source and served as the basis for the creation of many studies. This article is one of the first articles reflecting the linguopoetic essence of the word. In it, each word or language device can provide the appeal of the text when used in its place, instead of being a simple device for the text, to get hurt *and to get away* used *to express the same concept in two stories of the writer.* it is shown on the example of phrases, that they are used in their place according to the context of other words in the sentence and have a linguopoetic value. In the

---

[26]Mahmudov N. Linguistics of similes in Oybek's poetry.// Uzbek language and literature. - Tashkent, 1985. - #6. - B. 51.

article, the fact that the word has unlimited possibilities in the text, the skillful use of polysemy, formativeness, conflicting meaning and other phenomena creates unique artistic expressions is also analyzed on the basis of concrete examples. In the article , the linguopoetic factor is the product of the skillful use of language tools, and every *artistically* used language tool in the text can have a linguopoetic *value* . analyzed on the example of the use of the word. These thoughts show that any language tool that serves to reveal the writer's idea in an artistic text and is skillfully used will have linguopoetic value. In the article, all kinds of language tools, visual tools, unique syntactic structure of speech, folk constructions, characteristics of live speech, interconnection of sentences, sentence components, are a sign of the writer's artistic language skills and are a source for linguopoetic investigation [27].

I.Mirzaev, G.Muhammadjonova, D.Shodieva, M.Yakubbekova, M.Yoldoshev, G.Jumanazarova, Sh.Toshkhojaeva, S.Umirova, D.Turdalieva, D.Shodmonova also used linguopoetic analysis methods in their research [28]. The

---

[27]Mahmudov N. About the linguopoetics of Abdulla Qahhor's stories // Uzbek language and literature. -Tashkent, 1987. -#6. - B. 34-38.
Mirzaev I. Problems of linguistic and poetic interpretation of the poetic text. Autoref. ... diss. dr. Philol. science - Tashkent, 1992. Muhammadjonova G. Linguistic interpretation of Uzbek poetry of the late 80s and early 90s: Filol. science. name ... diss. autoref. - Tashkent, 2004; Shodieva D. Lingupoetics of Muhammad Yusuf's poetry: Philol.fanlari nomz. ... diss. autoref. - Tashkent,

study of the linguopoetic features of the language units in the text creates a basis for a broad illumination of the artistic-pictorial and emotional-expressive possibilities of the language. Only linguopoetic analysis serves to explain whether language means in a literary text are a linguistic unit or a connotative unit in the form of a simple nomema and to explain the artistic value of speech. In particular, while thinking about the artistic text, revealing the meaning of the tools that determine the artistic and the language units that create them is based on the linguopoetic analysis. This is the reason why this method is used more in the analysis of artistic discourse in Uzbek linguistics. Prof. While thinking about the function of language, N. Mahmudov emphasizes that the aesthetic function facilitates the communicative function of the language, and language and speech show expressiveness and power of influence precisely with the aesthetic function [29].

2007; Yakubbekova M. Linguistic features of Uzbek folk songs: Philol. doctor of science ... diss. autoref. - Tashkent, 2005; Yoldoshev M. Linguistics of literary text. - Tashkent, 2008; Jumanazarova G. Linguistics of the language of Fazil Yoldosh's epics: Philol. doctor of science ... diss. autoref. -Tashkent, 2017; Tashkho'jaeva Sh. Linguistics of Erkin A'zam's works. Philol. Ph.D. in philosophy. ... diss. autoref. – Fergana, 2017; Umirova S. Linguistic tools and poetic individuality in Uzbek poetry (as an example of Usman Azim's poetry): Philol. Ph.D. in philosophy. ... diss. - Tashkent, 2019; Turdialieva D. Linguistic features of Uzbek folk proverbs: Philology. Ph.D. in philosophy. ... diss. autoref. – Against, 2019; Shodmonova D. Linguistic features of Abdulla Oripov's poetry: Philol. Ph.D. in philosophy. ... diss. autoref. Against, 2019.
[29]Mahmudov N. Speech culture and the aesthetic function of language // Issues of Philology. - Tashkent, 2006, #2(11) -B. 47-51.

Demonstrating this aesthetic value of the language is based on the linguopoetic study of the artistic work. In the process of analysis, the artist's artistic skill is assessed by studying the artist's skill in using language, his own style, the choice of language tools and their use in accordance with the content of the artistic text. One of the first studies devoted to the linguopoetic study of the literary text is I.Mirzaev's doctoral dissertation on the linguopoetic problems of interpreting poetic texts [30]. In the research, specific linguopoetic features of poetic speech are analyzed on a linguopoetic basis: rhyme, the lexical structure of rhyme, the form and semantic features of words, dialectisms, and skillful use of foreign words for rhyming purposes. This research work is evidence that the linguopoetic analysis is a process with a wide object. That is, for this analysis, not only the use of words in the speech, but also artistic arts, visual means, and even the uniqueness of speech construction, if the textual structure of the speech creates expressiveness, can be an object.

One of the first researches in which poetic texts are analyzed from a linguopoetic point of view is G.Muhammadjonova's candidate thesis on the topic "Linguopoetic study of Uzbek poetry of the late 80s and early

---

[30]Mirzaev I. Problemy lingvopoeticheskoy interpretatsii stikhotvornogo texta. Autoref. ... diss. doc. f ilol. science – Tashkent , 1992.

90s" [31]. A characteristic feature of this research is the study of the linguopoetic nature of language tools in a specific type of speech, not of a particular creator. In the research, it is noted that the analysis of the language of the artistic work reveals the unlimited possibilities of the language, determines the value of the artistic work, evaluates the skills of a certain creator, determines the creative style, and takes an important place in the description of the literature of the period [32]. In this study, the word and its rhetorical value are discussed in artistic speech. Based on this goal, the linguopoetic possibilities of antonyms, homonyms, cognate words, individual neologisms, synonyms, historical words and other lexical tools in the Uzbek poetic speech of the late 80s and early 90s, figurative tools: revitalization, qualification, simile, metaphors, expressiveness of poetic speech , it is analyzed that it is an important tool that determines the pictoriality and imagery.

Analyzing Uzbek folk songs on a linguopoetic basis, M. Yakubbekova studied the fact that the most used visual tools in the text of folk songs: similes, metaphors, and adjectives are an important part of the art of folk songs. He emphasizes that his songs give an idea of the application of the principles of

---

[31]Muhammadjonova G. Linguistic interpretation of Uzbek poetry of the late 80s and early 90s: Filol. science. name ... diss. autoref. - Tashkent, 2004.
[32]Muhammadjonova G. Source indicated. - B. 6.

linguistic art [33]. In general, antithesis, synonyms, phrases, proverbs, repetitions, occasionalisms (D. Shodieva), phonetic means (phonepoetics), lexical means (lexopoetics), morphemic means (morphopoetics), grammatical means (Sh..Toshkho'jaeva), alliteration, parallelism, actualization and individuality (S.Umirova), folk proverbs (D.Turdialieva), metaphor (D.Shodmonova) were studied by such researchers.

The theoretical issues of linguopoetic analysis of artistic text in Uzbek linguistics are covered in the monograph "Linguopoetics of artistic text" by M. Yoldashev [34]. M. Yoldoshev compares the artistic text with the non-artistic text, and interprets the text whose purpose and essence is led by the aesthetic task as an artistic text [35].

Since the main purpose of creating an artistic text is to create an aesthetic effect, it is necessary to pay special attention to the relationship between certain parts in the overall structure of an artistic text, as well as emphasizing the importance of forming the content of expression, and shows that the writer uses a number of statements in the formation of the content. With this, the researcher draws attention to the need to take a broader approach to the issue of linguopoetic analysis of the

---

[33]Yakubbekova M. Linguistic features of Uzbek folk songs. Philol. doctor of science ... diss. - Tashkent, 2005, - B. 47.
[34]Yoldoshev M. Linguistics of literary text. - Tashkent, 2008.
[35]Yoldoshev M. Featured work. – B. 87;
Yoldoshev M. Source indicated. - B.104.

text, that is, to take into account the purpose of the writer to express the content. One of the important aspects of this research is that it presents the main principles of linguopoetic analysis. The unity of form and content of the artistic text, the unity of space and time, the universal language of the analyzed text, its various forms and relation to the literary language, the artistic-aesthetic integrity, approach to the artistic text as a whole, the identification of poetically actualized language tools in the artistic text, explicitness in the artistic text (open) and defines the principles of determining the implicit (hidden) ratio, determining the linguistic and semantic features of the mechanisms of intertextuality (intertextual communication) in the artistic text [36]. Relying on these principles is the basis of the linguopoetic analysis, and the study of explicitness and implicitness in the artistic text is an important part of the linguopoetic analysis from the point of view of the fact that it is an important feature of the artistic text, an artistic-aesthetic aspect. Because in artistic texts, tools that are often not expressed explicitly serve to provide artistic imagery, acquire an aesthetic essence. Accordingly, the research of explicit and implicit expressions, intertextuality, poetic actualization of language tools in artistic texts are important issues in the analysis of text linguopoetics. Linguistic analysis of the artistic

---

[36]Yoldoshev M. Linguistics of literary text. – Tashkent, 2008, - B. 150-159.

text should be a comprehensive analysis, in which not only linguistic tools, but also extralinguistic tools, which are the basis for creating the art of the work, should be researched from the point of view of aesthetic essence. After all, language in a work of art is related to other components of the work, including text structure.

The above-mentioned studies indicate that many scientific works related to the analysis of the language of artistic works have been created in Uzbek linguistics. At the same time, it should be noted that today's research dedicated to the study of the new Uzbek fiction language, which has a history of almost a hundred years, cannot be considered sufficient. Because the works of many leading creators of Uzbek literature have not yet become the object of linguistic research. Also, a number of works with special linguistic features are waiting for its researchers. One such creator is Murad Mohammad Dost. He is one of the mature representatives of Uzbek literature, his works show the rich possibilities of the Uzbek language. This situation requires the study of language features of Murad Muhammad Dost's works.

Textual structure and linguopoetic possibilities of Murad Muhammad Dost's works

The structure of the text in works of art is one of the main means of determining the artistic criteria of speech. The structure of the text is to convey the content of the work in a way that is convenient for the writer. This process takes place on the basis of the skillful use of the expressive possibilities of the language and the diversity of the expression method.

Literary texts, like other texts, are based on content expression, understanding, logic, and effectiveness of the text. Accordingly, in the artistic text, it is necessary to create various forms of text composition. The text and the style of expression in it clearly reflect the purpose of the writer, the idea he wants to convey and, finally, the skill of using language.

M. Yoldoshev, a scientist dealing with text problems, divides texts into two types according to their size and content. Texts are divided into minimum text (microtext) and maximum text (macrotext) according to the size symbol [37].

Composition of text according to content sign is an important part of artist's skill . After all, the textual structure of an artistic work also has an aesthetic effect based on the attractiveness of the expression, providing artistic effectiveness. The researcher of textual studies M. Yoldashev distinguishes

---

[37] Yoldoshev M. Fundamentals of literary text and its linguistic analysis. – Tashkent: Science, 2007. - B. 12.

seven types of texts according to their content and emphasizes that it is rare to find an artistic work based on only one of these types. The reason for this is that the artistic work has a very complex structure both in terms of composition and content, and it shows that all meaningful types of the text or some features of a certain type can be found in it [38].

Literary text is a type of text that differs from other forms of text, and it is diverse in terms of content. Because the artistic text is simple in terms of its linguistic construction in the content of reporting about ordinary events, it does not have artistic impact in terms of expression, it is different from the texts that reflect the ins and outs of everyday life, at the same time, it is rich in artistic expressions, descriptive texts, as well as narrative texts. is also organized. All types of texts in a work of art are interconnected and form one general text form, an artistic text.

Texts of works of art, regardless of their structure, are intended to have an aesthetic effect on the reader. Linguistic means are selected according to the content of the text. Text description is also derived from the content of the text. For example, narrative texts are based on a person's recollection of something from the past. Therefore, such texts are formed based on the appearance of monologic speech.

---

[38]Yoldoshev M. Linguistics of literary text. - Tashkent: Science, 2008. - B. 104.

The composition of a work of art is determined depending on whether it was able to organize the form elements in the work in the most optimal way to express the artistic content and realize the ideological-artistic intention [39]. The method of expression together with the appropriate use of language tools is important in the realization of the creator's ideological and artistic intention. The works of Murad Muhammad Dost stand out in terms of the uniqueness of such artistic expression. The author's works are unique in terms of textual structure, in which it is possible to observe different textual structures in terms of form and content. This situation is highlighted especially in the novel "Lolazor".

The first chapter of the work known as "The Patient" is distinguished by its textual character. This chapter is mainly composed of narrative text, based on the thoughts of the main character of the work, Nazar Yakhaboev. One of the unique aspects of the text can be seen in the composition of the text. The text is formed based on the speech of the author and the hero of the work. The author's speech is composed of an expression of the comment type, which consists of only two words. *He thinks and laughs* ("Lolazor"). After that, the hero's thoughts, based on his feelings and experiences, were the basis for the text. The structure of this text has the form of a

---

[39]Kuronov D. Poetics of shepherd's prose. - Tashkent, Sharq, 2004. - B. 254.

monologic internal speech. A characteristic feature of the text is that it is built on the basis of the thoughts of the hero. There is a reason for the character's thoughts. That is, *for a month, the nose scientist Fazil Salim Khan came with a bag of words that his teacher is a bad guy, your child had fun in Avvalbek's workshop, and then he asked me. He asked if we would study our father... later* ("Lolazor").

one phrase in this text is noteworthy. In this bag of words, there is also a boy's words that cause heartache. Accordingly, there is a bag of sentences *"a lot of speech"*, *"excessive speech"* and a sentence that affects the psyche of the hero of the work. By using this phrase in the text, the writer directs the hero of the work to think about the events that happened before.

This statement forces the hero of the work, Nazar Yakhaboev, to think about his child's attitude towards him, in connection with the events that happened before. These thoughts are a way of expression for the writer, they serve and determine the form of speech: *Yakshoboev knows that what Avvalbek said is a little different, that is, does he still read someone else's book after his death?* ("Lolazor")

This expression is also based on the thoughts of the hero of the work, and the thoughts of the hero's son's attitude towards him, the relationships in his family life earlier, based on these relationships, he had an allusion to the name of <u>*a dirty hoe*</u> and this allusion is expressed in the text by his son today. Between the text, the speech in the form of the author's word, the thoughts of the hero of the work based on his recollection, and the author's word continues.

The hero also imagines conversations with other people. In particular, conversations with the hospital's chief physician, the lame professor, pass through the hero's mind and a dialogical speech is created. This part of the work is mainly based on the thoughts of the hero. The last stanza of this chapter also ends with the protagonist's thought, which begins with *"thought is still pleasant."*

Noting that the interaction of the author's speech with the character's speech is one of the important features of the poetics of the prose work, Y. Solijonov admits that the inclusion of phrases characteristic of the character's speech in the author's narrative is more common in the works of Murad Muhammad Dost and Amon Mukhtar [40].

Don't rush, Yakshoboev, let's not rush, does he have to understand differently? There is a rare sincerity in his hatred, because Muhsina was hurt, she cried on the pillow for long nights. Sotok! Oh, sad insult!.. ("Lolazor")

These words are embodied in the mind of the hero. The reason for this is that his son used the term *"sassy taka"* against

---

[40]Solijonov Y. Speech and style. - Tashkent: Cholpon, 2002. - B. 39.

his father. In fact, this tashbeh is not his son's, but his wife Muhsina's. The thing that is taking shape in Yakhaboev's mind is that, in any case, his wife can use this allegory, she has hurt him even a little, but what about his son? Does his son have the right to say this? Yakshoboev uses *insulting* words to express his hatred . In this expression, the emotions and feelings of a person who looked back on his past life, reminisced about the past events, and did not see the light from his son, were expressed, and it was expressed in a form suitable for the content chosen by the writer.

Linguistic analysis of the novel "Lolazor" shows that the textual structure of the novel also depends on the lexical tools used in it. Therefore, the use of rude, rude words such as *aqpadar, sotak, sadqai insult and other similar words are not typical for the author's speech.* Accordingly, such words given in the work through the speech of the characters perform the task of individualizing the speech of the characters.

The main feature that distinguishes the novel "Lolazor" from other works is the way of expressing thoughts. This chapter in the novel, which begins with "The Patient", is a meaningful text, in which the hero remembers some past events (Sharif's death , *Haybatullah's failure to speak at the meeting, his wife Muhsina's phone call to Daminov,* "Lolazor"), through imagining his experiences. tells through

This style of expression is an individual way of expression related to the skill of the writer. This form of expression is typical for the novel "Lolazor". This method of expression continues in the second chapter of the novel known as "Kissanavis". This part is narrated in the form of a monologue based on one of the heroes of the work, Syedkul, who remembers and narrates the events that happened.

This part consists of a monologic text in which there is a dialogic speech (Saidkul and Yakhaboev's conversation). The writer's choice of a unique expression method for the intellectual construction of the work is also a sign of the artist's stylistic individuality. It is known that speech attractiveness and effectiveness are related to the use of speech tools, the use of visual tools, as well as the way of expressing thoughts.

The so-called "Patient" part of the novel could be represented otherwise, say, by telling someone the story, or by having a conversation with someone, or by the author's words. The writer uses a completely different method for expression, that is, the method of embodying the events that happened based on the thoughts of the hero. It is through this method that the inner world of the hero is revealed, his attitude towards others and his thoughts are clarified.

Through the words of the hero of the work of art, as well as in the texts where the opinion is expressed based on his thoughts on the events that happened before, the goal is to reveal the inner world of the person through his own words. This method is a traditional method of expression that is often found in works of art. The expression of thought through the imagination of the hero is a method that is rarely found in a work of art, and this expression is characterized by extraordinary effectiveness. This situation shows that one of the tools that increase the aesthetic value of an artistic text is the form of expression, that is, the structure of the text. M., - *Oh, you, you are an endless Nazar, I thought, one day Sharif's day will fall on you too?... So, at that moment, I remembered death, but not from death, but also from my companions. sitting on it, I was afraid that they would mock me as if they were mocking Sharif* ("Lolazor").

In the given text, it is expressed that the speaker drew conclusions from his own thoughts and blamed himself. This expression is also explained by remembering the event that has happened, by imagining it. This type of text is a narrative text in which an event heard or experienced is narrated. The peculiarity of the above text is that the event is not narrated in it, but imagined.

In this part of the work, there is a description of events such as the dialogue between Yakshoboev and the lame professor, Yakshoboev and Mrs. Muhsina, the conversation of Mrs. Muhsina with her son Olloyor, but all these events are expressed in the form of Yakshoboev's imagination and thoughts. It seems that the chapter of the work known as "The Patient" is a monologic speech that includes several dialogic speech in terms of speech structure. The second chapter of the book is called "Kissanavis". The "First scene", "Second scene" and "Third scene" parts of this chapter are also narrated in the language of the main character. The third chapter is again called "The Patient". In it, the images of the life of the main character Yakhaboev in the hospital are expressed, and it is unique in terms of its speech structure. At first, in this part, which is told from the language of the hero, the events embodied in Yakhaboev's thoughts are given: *Everything is in vain, Yakhaboev thought, now we are old, we don't have the strength to carry everything to the end. Now we need rest, let's summarize the past days, learn from the good ones, laugh at the bad ones, learn some lessons, and leave a valuable legacy to the heirs.* ("Lolazor")

In addition, this part also contains conversations between Yakshoboev and the chairman, Yakshoboev and Robiya, and this part also has the character of a monologic speech consisting of dialogic speeches in terms of its speech structure. Expression of expression in this way, on the basis of various forms of speech, is not found in the works of other writers. This case indicates that the novel "Lolazor" is a work with unique, original speech forms in terms of expression.

The fourth chapter of the novel is again called "Qissanavis" and begins with the narration of the hero of the work, Saidkul. The fourth, fifth and sixth scenes of this chapter are also narrated in the language of the hero and continue on the basis of a conversation between two people.

It is known that the main goal of a writer in composing a text is to draw the reader's attention to the story he is narrating, to awaken the reader's attitude to the work, thereby creating an aesthetic effect. Of course, the effect of the text on the reader is determined by the artistic and colorful expression of the thought, the richness of the language tools of the work, and the uniqueness of the expression method. In the novel "Lolazor", the novelty of the method of expression, the richness of the image, the clarity of the content were the basis for increasing the effectiveness of the work.

The main goal of the writer in a work of art is to tell a story about an event that happened to the hero. This process is reflected differently in different works. Sometimes the hero's life begins with the story of his youth, and the events until his old age are told in the language of the author or in the language of another character. Often, the direction of speech in such expressions is also the same, so such works often do not arouse interest in the reader. In the novel "Lolazor", first of all, the image of the life of the heroes alternates. The first part of the novel describes the subsequent life of the hero, while the second part describes the first periods of his life. Many events are narrated based on recollection of past events, and the speech patterns also vary. This method of telling the story saves the reader from boredom and increases his interest in the book.

One of the important features of the novel "Lolazor" is the uniqueness of the method chosen to reveal the character's inner world. The inner world of almost all characters is revealed through their speech. If the text of the work is analyzed from a content point of view, the text structure can be observed as follows.

of the work the main text is a text specific to the narrative genre . Because most of the work, especially in the parts known as "Qissanavis", the hero 's experiences or the events he witnessed are narrated. A part of the narrative text is told on the basis of recollection of the previous event. In the second and fourth chapters of the work, the text is expressed in the present tense, and in the sixth chapter, it is expressed in the past tense. In the text of the work, the narrative method leads. Although the opinion is mainly expressed in monologic speech style, it often switches to dialogic speech. Also, in this type of text in the work, there are many texts containing imagery and emotional expression. For example, *if you noticed, while describing our living conditions in Ortakurgan, I seemed to equate myself with brother Nazar and Oshon for a while.* Although the sixth chapter, known as "Kissanavis", begins with this text that has a narrative content, it also contains a text that expresses the content of the message: *If we are to be honest, I was very impressed with Yakhaboev at that time. Later, even when he took me a little closer to him, the dream in my heart did not dissipate even for a moment* ("Lolazor").

Emotional-expressive texts are of great importance in revealing the essence of a work of art. In this type of text, the inner feelings of a person are expressed in a unique way. Also, emotionally expressive texts are rich in imagery and artistic colors. Therefore, texts with emotional expression have a quick impact on the reader and evoke emotional pleasure.

In the works of Murad Muhammad Dost, there are many such texts and they serve to strengthen the artistic-imagery and impressiveness of the thought. The basis of works of art on more emotional and expressive texts is related to the provision of artistic imagery: *"The sky was shining from the standards." It was twenty years ago, it was autumn, and the sky was clear. And the cobwebs floated softly in the air, and a beautiful thought came to Nazar Yakhaboev's mind. As soon as it arrived, it settled in the heart, as if the end of a handkerchief had been tied into a knot* ("Lolazor").

This text is essentially an emotional text, and the expression, repetition of words, and representation of a figurative idea in it ensure the emotional impact of the text. From the criteria in this text, the image of the sparkling sky, the clear sky, the spider's threads, the floating of threads, and the images of tying a handkerchief will not leave the reader indifferent. Because the scene described in the text is artistic - colorful, rich in visual means. This situation can also be observed through the phrase " *he tied the end of the handkerchief in a knot"*. Because he buttoned the handkerchief, in fact, he put the thoughts that came to his mind in his heart, as if he was holding a handkerchief.

The writer Murad Muhammad Dost also has his place in Uzbek fiction and polishing language tools. The writer's works, especially the novel "Lolazor" are among the works that are perfectly prepared from the point of view of language, and are an example of the skill of using the national language. M.M.Dost's works are distinguished by their simple, fluent language, and at the same time, their impressiveness. It should be noted that the writer's works are among the works that make an important contribution to the development of the Uzbek literary language and the refinement of the artistic language in terms of language characteristics.

The characteristics of expression style and text structure in the novel "Lolazor" are also present in the writer's short stories "Resignation", "Return to Galatepa", "Mustafa". The text structure of these works is an example of the originality of the writer's method of expression, and the use of language tools is also related to the originality of the expression. M.M.Dost's works rarely use quiet, bookish words.

In "Return to Galatepa", whole pages, in "Resignation" many texts are expressed in the form of character's thoughts, so this style of text creation is the writer's individual style.

For this reason, the speech of the author and the hero of the work alternates in the writer's works. The writer's short story "Resignation" is distinguished in this respect. In this work, the statements are often expressed in the form of the character's thoughts based on inner speech. This method of expression can be called the leading method of expression in the works of M.M.Dost, and based on this situation, it can often be observed that the artistic effectiveness of the text is enhanced. For example, *Yakhaboev thought that now his wife is waiting for the elevator at the end of the corridor. After a while, he goes outside. On the street, behind the gate, Avvalbek is waiting with a car. This is not included. The head of the children is afraid of the father, aware of the fact that Salim Khan, the scholar, has arrived, he stands on the edge and waits for the ugly buck to lose his temper* ("Lolazor"). *He pressed his head to the pillow, we are so weak and small, Elomonov, he thought, look at how we walk and understand, a person who doesn't know might think that we are great! It's not a trifle, look, see, after living in the bright world for fifty-five years, did you finally expect this?! The result is very poor, Elomonov* ("Resignation"). These two quoted texts are close to each other in expression. In the first text, *Yakhasboev thought that the author's speech pressed his head on the pillow* in the second text, the rest of the thoughts appeared based on the characters' thoughts, all the words used in the text are typical of ordinary speech, and both texts are artistically perfect. In the first text, the things that are not in front of the eyes are imagined as being seen with the eyes, the attitude of the head of the children towards the father, especially when he calls him *an ugly bastard, does not leave the reader indifferent.* These expressions have factors that attract the reader's attention and influence him. In the second text, situations that show the hero's mentality, such as not being satisfied with oneself, questioning oneself, focusing on one's past life, and thinking about the consequences, do not fail to affect a person. Or *he looked at Cain and became strange. He thought that we could have taken him, he was playing, we didn't have any trouble... . No, it's not love, it's just that we feel sorry for Cain, his departure is also a good thing, when you show forced mercy, you'll feel sorry for yourself too ("Return to Galatepa")* is based on the feelings of the hero, thinking through his imagination, the leader in the writer's works expression is a method.

These expressions show that the expressiveness of the speech in the artistic text is created not only through language units and visual means, but also based on the way of expression of thought. An artistic text is, first of all, an example of an artistic image based on the method of expression. Accordingly, the text construction of an artistic work, various forms of speech expression can also be the object of linguopoetic analysis. After all, in any form of artistic expression, artistry is embodied to one degree or another.

The writer's skill in word choice and use

A work of art linguistically is comprehensive, it uses all vocabulary tools available in the national language, and as a result of the artist's skill in using words, it is directed towards expressing an impressive, figurative thought. The word is the main material of the artistic work, in the artistic work, images are created through words, and it reflects the general view of the world in the human mind. The most important features of the word, special aspects are shown in artistic texts. In a literary text, any word can be figurative, which shows the breadth of the word's pictorial potential. However, one of the main requirements for the realization of the wide potential of the word is the selective use of the word in speech. One of the important situations in the use of words in literary texts is that they are broken from the norm. Deviation from the norm in the use of words is an important aspect of artistic speech that shows the artistic-aesthetic essence, the main tool that increases the power of aesthetic impact. Linguistic study of M.M. Dost's works shows that the writer followed the following in choosing and using words.

1. Finding and using a word that matches the essence of the thought to be expressed, expresses the meaning in a clear and understandable way.

2. Avoiding silence in expression, expressing thoughts through sentences that are easily accepted by the people. To do this, choose words that are used by the general public and whose meaning is understood by everyone.

3. To express the thought in artistic colors, to use the nuances of the word's meaning and artistic richness.

4. Using emotional-expressive words that serve to ensure effectiveness in speech in accordance with the direction of speech.

5. Effective use of the possibilities of expressing the meaning of synonyms at different levels and in different colors.

6. Appropriate use of the features of the expression of different meanings of words.

7. Selection of lexical tools that do not conform to the norms of formal artistic language, but have a wide possibility of organizing artistic expressiveness.

An important aspect of artistic speech is that a word combines with other words to express meaning, and the word organizes the attractiveness and diversity of the speech with this aspect. The range of expressiveness of a lexical tool expands according to its semantic and logical connection with another lexical tool. Words express an additional meaning in the text in addition to the lexical meaning and create stylistic possibilities according to these meanings. Due to the constant communication between speech styles, a word characteristic of a certain speech type is transferred to another speech type. Artistic speech is opened on the basis of such a connection and relationship between words and words, the use of words and the manifestation of various characteristics of words. This case shows that when using a certain word in speech, the demand of other words in the speech is also important. Because the use of any word in the text is related to the style of the writer, the manifestation of the meaning and stylistic possibilities of the word depends on the text. Any text structure, in terms of the use of lexical and methodological tools in it, shows the uniqueness of the individual style of the text creator. The individual style of the writer is the basis of his artistic skill. Through the skill of individual use of words, the essence of the artistic work is revealed and artistic impression is created. Accordingly, the artist's artistic skill is primarily determined by the purposeful use of language tools in the process of artistic expression.

The works of Murad Muhammad Dost are considered as important sources that show individuality in the use of words. This situation can also be observed in the example of the expression of one situation through several linguistic means in the writer's work. In particular, the writer uses unique individual expressions to express happiness and sadness, which represent the human state of mind. For example, " *It's enough, Tashpolat brother, stop it,*" *said Zamira bitterly, but she didn't get angry, she turned her face away trying to hide the laughter that landed on her lips* ("Return to Galatepa"). This text, which describes a state of mind, uses the combination *of laughter to express the concept of happiness* . This expression could also be given with the combination of *hiding his happiness* . In this case, the idea that the writer wanted to express would lose its artistic color and become a simple expression.

  D.N. Shmelev, thinking that artistic expression requires expressive-imagery, often considers metaphors, epithets, similes, repetitions and other tools as providing imagery, but artistic text should not contain figurative metaphorical words, expressions, but the text should be expressive-stylistic admits that it is possible [41].

  Murad Muhammad Dost used both metaphorical and non-metaphorical expressions to express the concept of happiness. For example, *Elpinish decreases, the air in the room seems to cool down, the clouds on the face disappear* , and the mood *improves* .

---

[41]Shmelev D.N. Words and image. - M.: Nauka, 1964, p. 38.
Vasilyeva A.N. Artistic speech. - Moscow, Russian language, 1983, p. 52.

The provision of expressive coloring of the artistic text without metaphorical expressions is related to the artist's skill in using words. Because any word has the characteristics of creating certain stylistic possibilities in the text. Especially in the process of combining with other words, the expansion of the expressive features of the word is the basis for the emergence of new, original expressions.

defines a word combination as a combination of images, a molecule with a unique image formed from the atoms of words and images.[42]

In the works of Murad Muhammad Dost, one can find many such word combinations, characteristic of the writer's individual style. It is characteristic that the writer creates many options of figurative means in expressing one concept and enhances the artistic and colorfulness of the text. For example, *But alas, the guest is greater than your father, I hurried to the prospect of Yakhaboev with a smile on my face.* "joy" in the sentence ("Lolazor") To express the meaning, the combination of *khuraram and rub on the face* is used. In these texts, the use of two expressions, such as ``to *put a smile on the lips" and* ``to *put a smile on the face", to express the same concept, shows how wide the language has in choosing and using words.* The wealth of language tools of the speech is related to the skill of

---

[42]

the writer's choice of words. Expressing the concept with different means in artistic texts, using different linguistic means to express different levels of the same concept shows the limitless possibilities of the language, but the means of expressing the subtle meaning of the language are often created on the basis of creative skills.

The selection of new means of expression, which are not readily available in the language, and their appropriate use in their place provides individuality. Murad Muhammad Dost is a unique creator in terms of choosing words and using them in speech. While thinking about the shepherd's language skills, prof. M. Yoldoshev writes: "One of the advantages of highly skilled writers in terms of artistic language is that they do not only use ready-made meaningful words that exist in the language, but also use non-meaningful words according to the needs of the artistic image in such a way that these words are perceived in the text in the same way as meaningful words. "[43]. We will not be mistaken if we say that these thoughts apply to the work of M.M.Dost. Because in the writer's works, there are many lexical units in the form of word combinations created by such a creator and showing the wide possibilities of the language, and the use of such language units formed the writer's style of language use. An important aspect of the writer's skill is

---

[43] Yoldoshev M. Secrets of the word shepherd. - Tashkent: Spirituality, 2002. - B. 16.

the skillful use of the resources of the national language. In his works, using the words existing in the language and the meanings expressed by these words, unique word combinations are created and new meanings are expressed.

One of the important features of works of art is the possibility of using the word in other meanings, which are not characteristic of the original dictionary meaning. The orientation of the word to express such other meanings shows the expressiveness of the language, the scope of the artist's linguistic skill in using words. While Murad Muhammad Dost expressed the meaning of *"joy" with the words "to put a smile on the lips" and "to put a smile on the face" , he* was able to create an original word combination to express the opposite meaning of *"sadness"* . *Yakhaboev became alert, wiped the smile from his face and became sad* ("Lolazor"). As a result, in the writer's work, expressions of the concepts of *happiness and sadness* have been created, which create conflicting meanings: *to rub a smile on the face and to make one laugh* .

Prof. that the individuality of the work of art is an important factor determining the artistic value of the work. This is how S. Karimov explains. "The creator perceives the material world in his own way, he can see the aspects of things and events in nature and society that no one has noticed, so that what we say is common for everyone in consumption - language becomes a tool of individual image in the writer's pen. That's why every work of art is truly private [44]. " In fact, the originality of the artist's perception of the material world and its expression creates specificity. Specificity is not created by the use of common semantic features of the language like everyone else, but on the contrary, it is created by the writer as a result of new meanings, new expressions that do not exist in the common language. For example, *Lang opened the windows. In the sentence "Lolazor", the birds that started the meeting in the trees flew away,* the incessant chirping of the birds on the branches of the tree is figuratively expressed through the word combination *that started the meeting* . Expressing a specific meaning through this combination, the writer compares the singing of birds with argumentative meetings, and as a result of the connection between these situations, the word combination that started the meeting was used.

The originality of the use of words in a work of art is related to the perception of the creator. If the creator imagines a thing-phenomenon in connection with another thing-phenomenon, he expresses the previous situation with a word representing the imagined concept. For example, *Today's friend is tomorrow's enemy, to smear mud on someone else's face in order to keep myself spotless... Yes, there were many such... There were many of today's enlightened old men who could not*

---

[44]Karimov S. Artistic style of the Uzbek language. - Samarkand: Zarafshan, 1992. -B. 26.

stop their hands that were not covered with mud in the saying ("Lolazor") The use of the words "*slap mud*" and "*mud load*" are characteristic in this respect. *Mud slinging,* used as an expression of the meaning of *"accusation",* is not just an accusation, but an unjust accusation, an accusation made for one's own benefit. In expressing these meanings, no other lexical device is as suitable and artistically colorful as the combination of *mud-slinging*. This case is an example of the writer's great skill in choosing and using words. The combination of *slurping* exists in the vernacular and has the characteristic of expressing the meaning used in the text. Based on the connection between the denotative meaning and the connotative meaning of this combination, the writer also uses the combination of mud-laden hand. In both usages, the meaning of the compounds was formed on the basis of a transfer of meaning, expressing a new concept and creating an individual style. The manifestation of new expressive aspects of language tools can be observed based on the writer's use of the combination of *threshing and heaping*. *Threshing* is used colloquially in grain farming and means *"gathering the stalks or grains together"*, based on this concept there is a meaning of *"plurality"*. The writer uses the same semantic features of the combination in the vernacular language to provide speech tone by using the combination of *threshing* against the proliferation of false praises. *Lutfi threshed donations so much that*

Yakhasboev's faith was left behind ("Lolazor"). In the use of this combination to express a certain meaning, there is also a hint of the falsity of the praises being uttered. The person to whom the compliments are directed knows this. The writer skillfully reflected this situation through the words of *a bahya zabi*.

There are different ways and different tools that show the artist's skill in using words. One of the important indicators of vocabulary skills is the creation of new words and their use in the context of the text.

Word creation occurs only in the process of artistic speech, but not all writers' works contain newly created words. Therefore, word formation is related to the individual style of the creator.

If the creation of new words is based on the internal capabilities of the language, some of them may adapt to the norms of the literary language and become popular, while some creations may remain specific to a particular speech. In both cases, the newly created text is either used for a naming task or aimed at performing a methodological task.

Accordingly, it is important to study the author's creation of new words and their effective use in determining the uniqueness of the lexicon of an artistic work. The writer Murad Muhammad Dost, as a talented writer, followed in the footsteps of great wordsmiths, was able to create new words and skillfully use them in his works. It is possible to observe cases where the writer used some patterns of word formation existing in the language in the formation of new words.

It is observed that the writer strictly adheres to the word formation norms of the language, using the internal capabilities of the language in creating new compositions in his works. Therefore, the new constructions found in the writer's works are natural and consistent with the nature of the language. For example, *E, live together with your elder, thinks Yakhaboev, is it possible to recover from such nervousness! The formation of the word "nervous"* in the sentence ("Lolazor") is also individual according to the essence of the content. This word, meaning *"nervousness", "touching a nerve",* is unique in its usage. As a great word artist, the writer relies on active patterns of word formation using the language's capabilities and creates new words based on existing word formation patterns.

word *nervousness* has the word-forming suffixes *-boz* and *-lik , and the word is formed twice. The suffix -boz* is used to make nouns with the meaning of dealing a lot with things (doorman, gambler) as well as being too devoted to things (housekeeper, trickster). In the word *"Asabboz"* , these meanings are not so noticeable, and it is observed that the writer created the possibility of expressing a new meaning of the suffix. In other words, this word in the text is not used in the main meaning of the suffix *-boz , that is, to deal with things a lot, but rather in the sense of "breaking the nerve".* It seems that in the formation of this word, not the traditional meaning of the artificial base was used, but the possibilities of expressing a new meaning were used, and the extent of the possibility of word formation in the language was demonstrated. Such tools reflecting the writer's skill in using words can be found in many works of Murad Muhammad Dost. Another one of such individual creations is the word *gossip* : *"If I say, it would be gossip, domlajan,"* said Chorshanbiev, blushing .

"You're right, it's good that you didn't do anything petty." We are wolves, Wednesday boy, we don't know what to whisper ("Lolazor").

The word *communication is not used in the sense of "notifying"* , but in the sense of *"conveying"* . According to this expression, this word is completely new. This word is unique due to the nature of its formation. Although it was made on the basis of *the noun + kash pattern* existing in the language , the meaning of the suffix *"to pull" in the language* was weakened, and the activation of the meaning of *conveying* was the basis for creating a new word. A completely different situation can be observed in the word *"smallness"* formed on the basis of *quality + cache* . This word is also characteristic of the writer's style and has an occasional character. The fact that the meaning of this word expressed in this text cannot be expressed by another word in the language shows the uniqueness of the creation of this lexical tool. In the text, the word pettiness is used to express such meanings as *"being superior to others", "not engaging in gossip", "not carrying small talk"* . In addition, this word system also expresses the meaning of possessing characteristically good traits. On the basis of both constructions - *the* suffix kash has formed a personal noun meaning to deal with something expressed from the base, to perform an action through this base. Taking into account the possibility of rapid absorption into the language from the point of view of the constructional basis, constructions of this type are characterized by the emergence of a lexical tool that creates the possibility of expressing a new meaning for the language.

It can be observed that the writer derives from the meaning of the root word in this type of word formation. As a result, clarity and vitality were reflected in the interpretation of expression in the new production. The basis of the word *communication* is message. However, this word represents a simple message about an event. The writer assigns the function of style to the new creation made by this word. That is, the word is used in the meaning of *"to make a joke", "to convey a message" and not just to convey a message . The word subtlety is similar* in meaning to the word *intelligence* . It is noticeable that these words are used very appropriately in the text.

In addition to being a lover of literature, the writer is a selfless creator who uses language tools carefully and is able to make wide use of the available opportunities in the language.

The writer's frequent appeal to the rich stylistic tools of the national language, ensuring the attractiveness of the language of his work through these tools, vividly embodies his attitude to the language. In the new creations found in the works of Murad Muhammad Dost, it is possible to observe the same stylistic coloring, the expression of new meanings that do not exist in the language.

In the formation of new words, the rules of word formation are strictly observed. The creation of new words in artistic creation is the result of natural and creative needs. The nature of the artistic image requires the use of many unexpected, unnatural new expressions in it, which makes it possible to create new words in the artistic text.

Whether the new creations remain in the originally used text or become active and pass into the common language depends on the existence of the basis of word formation in the common language and the extent to which the meaning of the new coined word can express the people's lifestyle. If there is no convenient, simple, understandable word for expressing certain concepts representing people's life, or if the word expressing a certain concept does not exist in the language, a new artificial language expressing that meaning becomes popular. In this respect, a number of designs found in Murad Muhammad Dost's works are characteristic. It can be observed that some of the creations found in the writer's works serve as synonyms for vocabulary tools expressing certain concepts, while some of them appear as completely new words. For example, - *Is this a hospital or a caravanserai? he asked. - Let's come in as soon as I get hung up?* The word " interrogated " in the sentence ("Lolazor") is a word specific to the writer's individual style. As an expression of the meaning of this word, the word "asked" is used in the common language. As long as a language has a word that expresses a particular meaning, the creation of a new word has an intended purpose. That is, the level of meaning expression of a certain word is the extent to which it expresses the idea that the writer wants to express, or to withdraw from the same expressions based on the multiplication of words with the same meaning in the language, to provide speech diversity, to impose the task of expressing an additional meaning on the word, to use the word in a completely new sense, to create new creations in speech. will be the basis. If the word *"asked"* used in the above text is approached from this point of view, it can be understood that it is used as a synonym of the word *"asked"* , but not exactly as a word *"asked"* . The text means *"to ask a question"* explains that it is used in the sense that it is a new word and an original usage. *"ask a question"* **The use of the word** *"asked"* in the sense of "asked " is the creation of a new word in the language, the lexical enrichment of the language.

It seems that an important aspect of using words in speech, especially the use of words with a new meaning, is the manifestation of meaning facets that are expressed in addition to the main meaning. Murad Muhammad Dost also chooses words to express such subtle meanings and creates new words. *Gaybarov noticed his intention and shook his head (* "Return to Galatepa"). The word *"nod"* is a new word that expresses the common colloquial meaning of *"he shook his head"* . Sorting the head is a sign of expressing different human states. In the sentence quoted above, this word expresses disapproval of the interlocutor's opinion. *Zamira shook her head regretfully, biting her lips and exited the pit* ("Return to Galatepa"), and the word *"discontent"* is expressed by this word. The characteristics of the word to express such subtle meanings become a means of artistic expression for the writer. By using the word *"sarakladi" which* means "to move the head", the artist managed to express his idea in a new form that was not expressed before.

Murad Muhammad Dost uses new word forms that do not exist in many languages in order to create a new form of expression, sometimes to express a new meaning in his works. For example, кубалаб, which means *"to pass the button"* (*They went out. The cold hit his face. Elamonov paused and buttoned his coat.* "Resignation"), *archeologist in the sense of dealing with the sciences of history, archeology (- Who, he, Gaybarov, is a walking old scholar.* "Return to Galatepa"), ishqnama *in* expressing the meaning of *" romantic letters"* . meritorious in expressing the meaning (*In the credits of those films, the names of some meritorious and needy young men were also included. If he uses the words "Lolazor"),* he uses the combination of *"guest ",* which is one of the best traditions of our people, to express the custom of inviting people from neighbors and relatives to the house to honor them when distinguished guests come to the house. . *It is true that they put the izat in its place, they bring the whole family to the owner, behind the owner, showing the guest* ("Return to Galatepa"). It is also *a mature demand* for artistic style (*Panzhi is a thief, and since he tied a belt around his waist, Ahil's khovlikma pishang talak, which is like open power, has not pleased the people.* "Return to Galatepa"), *table (The heart is touched by their melody, and Gaybarov's tune, sitting by the window of the car, nods at the table.* "Return to Galatepa"), *I built a house like a building by messing with my friends.* " Lolazor ", cooler (*A comfortable office with wide ceilings, comfortable furniture, double windows with double frames, one air conditioner in each window humming and working, he couldn't believe his eyes.* "Resignation"), *kamyurim (Mustafa is a hard-working man, unless he is very shy, he smiles a lot from home.* "Mustafa"), as well as *"this is* what we will become" (*-I will not grow, - says Hamrakul. -This is what we have become, bro.* "Mustafa") and *"to speak" It is used* to express the meaning (*"They are still there, Salimboy," he says. "He has a lot of strength, but he has little intelligence.* "Mustafa") are used to reveal the writer's purpose and to express the subtle aspects of the thought, not just to use words. , but approaching it as an artistic use of words helps to analyze the writer's skill in using language.

An important characteristic of Murad Muhammad Dost's artistic style is the special emphasis on certain aspects of expression. In such cases, the writer increases the artistic effectiveness of the thought based on the use of words' proximity, meaning, negative or positive meaning in order to increase expressiveness, expressiveness. The writer also chooses words for this form of expression. The writer's works often use a series of words to express the thought with all its subtlety, to explain the correctness and accuracy of the thought to be expressed. The listener's attention is drawn to the thought based on the successive use of words that complement each other in terms of expression, the importance of the thought to be expressed is emphasized, and the artistic coloring of the thought is ensured. For example, ... *this comrade is a person worthy of the times, honest, clean, smart and an entrepreneur, I am happy to work side by side with this comrade.* In the phrase "Lolazor", four characteristics of a person are distinguished as a sign of appropriateness for the times: honesty, purity, wisdom and entrepreneurship. When expressing these signs, the words honest, pure, smart, entrepreneur are used, which show the good qualities of a person. In this sentence, one of the above signs could be used to reflect the person's suitability for the times.

However, the writer does not determine the appropriateness of the times by one positive characteristic in a person, he emphasizes that such persons have several positive characteristics and gives a series of words indicating these characteristics. It seems that a series of words that are close to each other in terms of general expression is also a means for the writer to express the idea vividly. When words that are close to each other in terms of their general meaning are used in the text, the meaning of each of them is highlighted separately, as a result, the expressiveness of the expression increases again. For example, *But the dark seeds were left aside, and millions of hectares were sown with seeds from the same field, because the owners of the field are better, more influential, more dirty, more ugly, paler, dirtier than others... ("Lolazor")* . In this sentence, all the words aimed at attracting the attention of the reader express a negative attitude in terms of content, even the words excellent, prestigious, which have a positive color according to the meaning of the word, have acquired a negative meaning in the text, through these words, "a person who does what he says" in the text . the meaning of the word is expressed and the word acquires a negative meaning also shows the writer's skill in using words. Because these words cannot express a positive meaning surrounded by words with a negative meaning. The expression of a common meaning from organized fragments is the law of language. Another important indicator of a writer's skill is the increasing degree of punctuation in a string of words. A clear proof of this *is more stained - more vile - paler - dirtier* A word characterized by a higher negative color in a string of words *is dirtier* is the word. In his writings, the writer attached special importance to this method of expression, bringing the word acceptable to him to the end of the sequence of words and assigning the main meaning to this word. For example, *That's why I was snoring like a hen's cock - serious, dignified, dignified!* ("Resignation"). In this sentence, because the word *vygorli is a word* that expresses the sound of a chicken walking like a rooster, it is taken at the end of the sentence and directed to express the main meaning. In the text, a man is compared to a rooster, but although the rooster does not have the seriousness and strength characteristic of a man, there is a similarity in the way a rooster and a man walk with dignity. This situation was the basis for the artist to express his artistic and pictorial opinion by comparing two subjects.

    The possibilities of language tools expand even more in such expressions of opinion based on the comparison of subjects. Although all three words in the quoted sentence are mainly representative of human characteristics, in this text they also served for art by expressing certain situations in the rooster. This situation shows that there are many tools and methods that serve the art in the language. Every artist uses this treasure in his own way and expresses his artistic and impressive ideas.

One of the important methods of word usage is the sequential use of semantically close words typical of Murad Muhammad Dost's works. Emphasis is strengthened through this method, and several characters in the object or event are highlighted separately. For example, *Uncle Murad was born from the depths of memories, as dear, pure and simple as the memory itself.* The sentence ("Return to Galatepa") also shows skill in the use of words. First of all, the characteristics characteristic of the person were emphasized, thereby the person was evaluated. Secondly, it is expressed that these characteristics belong not only to the person, but also to his memories, that is, the memories of a person are also dear to him, pure and simple. It seems that in this text too, the word is directed towards expressing a double meaning. In the first case, when attributed to a person, it appeared in a denotative function based on relevance, and in the second case, when attributed to memory, it performed a connotative function as a product of the writer's way of thinking. Academician I. Kochkortoev thinks that the word is the material for creating an image and scene in fiction, and notes that it is the writer's skill to find words that vividly express a certain action, scene and situation in life and use it in accordance with the idea of the work, the spirit and logic of the image [45]. B. Yoldoshev explains the manifestation

---

[45]Kochkortoev I. Stylistics of artistic speech. - Tashkent: Teacher, 1976. - B.

of language tools in an artistic work on the basis of three relational units as follows:

a) attitude to objects and events in reality;

b) attitude to the speaker's, person's dreams, feelings, thoughts;

possession of the characteristic of naming, showing and aesthetic evaluation of [46]a specific object, event . It seems that the word used in the artistic text has many speech functions, as well as wide possibilities of meaning expression. As these opportunities in the word are manifested in the expression of meaning, in the creation of an image, this situation is influenced by other words in the speech. In this sense, the use of words with close meanings that define Murad Muhammad Dost's style can be evaluated as a way to reveal the writer's goal and idea. This method creates a unique artistic tone for the writer, and the artistic-aesthetic essence of the text increases. For example, *there is a wild man standing on top of ..., monkey-like, hairy and tall, and so on* ("Lolazor") . *Hairy, tall, impressive* used in the text words are related to the word *monkey* . On the basis of interpretation of monkey quality, the following words are used, which ensures the tone of the speech, creates imagery as a representative and qualifier of the situation, and enhances the

---

27.
[46]Yoldoshev B. Learning the language and style of a work of art. Issues of Uzbek language stylistics and speech culture. - Samarkand, 1980. - B. 49 - 50.

speech effectiveness. Accordingly, it is necessary to evaluate the use of this word as a choice of words suitable for the essence of the speech, the writer's skill in using words. In the following sentence, it can be observed that the writer chose words according to the content of the text. *All the people seen are calm, there is no expression on their faces, except for the noise of the stream, everything is peaceful, quiet, without noise* ("Lolazor"). The words *"Osuda"*, *"peaceful"* and *"no noise"* describe tranquility, *so there is no hadik on people's faces.* This sentence also expresses the proportionality of the word in the process of expressing meaning with other words in the speech. It is observed that this method of using words is used in order to emphasize what is considered important in the process of expressing the writer's opinion, to attract the opinion. For example, *a two-way family is not a family, but a vessel with cracks and boundaries, boundaries, shelter, livelihood, income, expenses, children's worries* ("Resignation"). The comparison of a double-tracked family to a bounded container is an example of artistic thinking, applying the combination of double-tracked to a family that does not have a defined direction (path) in managing a creative family, and compares such a family to a narrowed container. These limits are: shelter, livelihood, income, expenses and concern for children, which are an integral part of human life. In order to fully express the essence of this strong logical idea, the writer uses words that complement each other in meaning, in order to express an attractive and impressive idea. Commenting on the artistic text as an artistic-aesthetic whole, Professor M.Yoldoshev writes: understanding is possible as a result of spiritual-cultural, intellectual-emotional and linguistic-aesthetic activity" [47]. By this, the scientist means the complexity of the perception of the artistic text, the manifestation of the meanings of the language tools found in it in an open and hidden way. Because the variety of language tools in artistic works, the use of figurative and polysemous words, the cases of expressing subtle meanings based on synonyms require that the content of the text is in most cases internal. This situation prevents the correct understanding of the content of the text and the full understanding of the meanings of the words used in it. Since the language of the works of the writer Murad Muhammad Dost is close to the national language, although there are meaningful expressions in it, signs of simplicity and superficiality are noticeable, and it is not difficult to understand the text and understand the ideas in it. This situation is determined by the writer's special attention to language tools and the use of words in their common language meanings. Expressing attractive thoughts using such simple words is an example of the writer's skill. *Suddenly, his body was filled with anger. But this feeling had no strength, was weak,*

---

[47]Yoldoshev M. Linguistics of literary text. - Tashkent, 2008. - B. 27.

strange, poor. He had a bad heart. The same can be seen in the use of the words *"weak", "garib" and "benavo"* in the sentence ("Lolazor") . The consecutive use of these words is also based on the purpose of drawing attention to the existing situation and emphasizing it.

In general, a writer has a unique style of word choice and usage. Although all parts of this study reflect on the writer's use of words, it should be emphasized that creating a new word, strengthening the artistic-aesthetic essence of the thought based on the consecutive use of words with common meaning is a unique aspect of the writer's use of words.

IN THE WORKS OF MURAD MUHAMMAD DOST AS A TOOL FOR PROVIDING THE INDIVIDUALITY OF THE WRITER OF WORDS

M.M. Dost individual in his works means of speech

In linguistics, studies devoted to the study of the language of an artistic work into historical-etymological layers, based on the division of the language, are rare. There are specific reasons for this: First, research in the nature of analysis of the lexical layer of the language is not important for an artistic work.

Secondly, the word used in an artistic work is determined not by its source, but by its function in the speech process. Therefore, in determining the artist's ability to use words, not only which languages he uses words, but how they are used appropriately plays an important role. Prof. A.I.Efimov explains the lexical richness of the language of artistic works as follows and notes that they can be divided into the following lexical groups: a) journalistic lexicon; b) artistic-poetic lexicon; professional and technical terms; words related to official work [48].

It seems that the language of the artistic work is lexically diverse, and therefore there are different ways of studying the

---

[48] Efimov A.I. Stylistics of artistic speech. - M.: 1961. -S. 206
Vinogradov V. About the language of fiction. - M., 1959. -S. 7

language of the work in linguistics. Including Acad. V. Vinogradov emphasized that in studying the lexical features of the artistic work, it is necessary to approach based on the function of the words in the speech process [49]. The critical importance of this type of analysis for language investigators is recognized in all studies. However, the analysis of the language of an artistic work only from a stylistic point of view limits the study of other lexical tools that do not perform a stylistic function in the work, but provide artistry. Accordingly, if the study of the language of an artistic work is approached based on the function of the used language tool, taking into account all the linguistic tools in it, it is possible to reveal all the features of the language of the artistic work. The study of the language of M.M. Dost's works was also approached from this point of view, and the linguistic tools used in the writer's works were analyzed to reveal the specific features of the artistic text.

It is known that the word is an important tool that expresses the basis of the speech, as well as the artistic work. Consequently, writers create images by using words, express natural scenes, characters, their inner feelings and experiences with the help of words. Therefore, the most important tool for a work of art is the word and its use. Accordingly, a writer's skill is also largely determined by his use of language. After all,

---

[49] Vinogradov V. About the language of fiction. - M., 1959. -S. 7

artistically colorful, impressive, figurativeness of the work is based on skillful use of language tools.

A work of art expresses a way of life. And the way of life is different. In life, there are people living in different places, whose character and characteristics are completely different from each other. The complexity of this process is that they are selected, summarized on the basis of their common features, and brought into a work of art. This requires great skill from the writer, and in such cases, an individual speech is created in a work of art. Murad Muhammad Dost's works are based on such an individual speech, and each character's unique speech is created.

For example, one of the heroes of the work is Hotam Shura, the chairman of the village council, who has put all his efforts into the creation of innovation for development. He burns his soul only for development: To express these characteristics in Hotam Shura, the writer uses the following words: people-loving, patriotic, but lazy, accustomed to the treatment of the village, a unique person. Therefore, when describing Hotam Shoro, the writer treats him with respect and describes all his features through his speech and words: *Hotam Shoro looked at the faces of the brigadiers for a moment, and felt sorry for the fact that, like two gray-haired young men, they did not move forward to the distant city and the near future. he wanted to say good things, he wanted to be comforted, but he did not notice that completely different words came out of his mouth.* ("Lolazor") Through this expression, the writer expressed his sympathy for Hotam Shoro, one of the heroes of the work. The use of words and phrases such as *pity, good words, comfort* in this sentence indicates that the hero of the work is actually a good human being.

pity for those who did not advance towards the near future in the text is characteristic. It is this state of pity that causes Hotam Shura to express other thoughts, not the thoughts that passed through his heart. Because he would like these tired people to strive for the improvement of their life and lifestyle, to strive for the future like the young men who went to the city to study. Sensing that they do not have such desires, the words of the chairman remain in his mind, and other words come to his tongue: - *Thinking that the chairman is sick, you all went crazy! You drive two oxen, and you don't drive one man of land! Look at the poor field until you are stuck in your wife's idol, if the field does not give birth, what your wife gave birth to will die of hunger, you bastards! Where is Norma? Where did you put Normat, Normatboy? What about you, nurse Eshmat, don't you go out to the field a little earlier before you hear the sound of pants? I will still show you my mother* ("Lolazor").

This text of Hotam Shura's speech contains only insults. Vulgar words and phrases are used in it , such *as to run away, to stick to the wife's idol, nomardlar, where did you put the norm, nanny, and to lie down like a pant* . The text consists of threatening content. This text is built on the basis of simple colloquial speech tools. The words in it have an emotional color, which ensures the artistic impact of the text. These sentences, which at first glance seem very rude, convey an idea that is not too harsh, and does not even offend the listener. This is the result of the writer's skill in choosing characters, creating their own language, as well as using the universal language. After all, Hotam Shoro was actually a " *poetic person, even when he spoke, he sounded drowsy, finished a song, spoke like a lively storyteller, and even used to sing to the brigadiers* ." These are the reasons why Hotam Shura's rude speech in terms of form does not have a bad effect on people. He lost a leg in the war, he is a man who lives for the sake of the people and thinks that people's lives will improve, so everyone respects him even when he insults him.

One of the characteristics of the novel "Lolazor" is the use of vulgar words. In the novel , many insulting words such as *sassik taka, goringda donguz kopgur, aqpadar, sadqai moylov, megajin, manjalaki, er so-called hezalak, cursed shah, muguzdaru gaddor, landovur, anoyi, anqov, soft broom, yasuman are used to express the attitude towards people.* . The language of the work is lexically close to the common colloquial language. Complex, bookish language tools are rare in it. It seems that the writer deliberately tries to use the form of the vernacular in expressing his artistic opinion and chooses the simple colloquial form of the vernacular to ensure the comprehensibility and effectiveness of the language of the work. This situation, characteristic of the narrative of the play, can be found in the speech of all the characters.

In particular, as a means of highlighting the character of one of the characters of the work, Jonuzok Karvan, the following simple colloquial words that appear in his speech were used: *bale, chatog', ekkan, my obligation* . These language tools express his unique speech, and through the speech of another character in the novel, Simkho, his nationality is expressed: " *Hey Saidqul brother, don't talk like that!" he said. Simho is hurt. - If they hear it, you will be upset! - Those who joined first, then those who left! But the authorities are left!* ("Lolazor").

Words such as say, don't talk, bisyar khaba, meshad, badaz, and aftorityot mentioned in Simho's speech indicate the simplicity of the language of the work and the fact that it is expressed in the form of the vernacular. In fact, the main characteristic of the language of the work is linguistic simplicity. In the speech of all the characters in the work, you can find such folk expressions, words characteristic of ordinary speech, that it can be interpreted that the writer chose this form in artistic expression in order to ensure artistic richness. After all, the heroes of the work are also ordinary, and some of them even have stupidity. Such a feature is present in the main characters of the work, Nazar Yakhaboev and Saidkul, which is the basis for choosing a simple colloquial form of language for the writer's expression. Secondly, it should be noted that the use of literary-literary words is the main criterion for a work of art, because linguistic tools of this type are the main lexical units that increase the artistic effectiveness of speech. Such words are distinguished, first of all, by their figurativeness. The elements of ordinary colloquial speech are stronger than literary-book words in providing artistic coloring through the richness of such imagery. These features of lexical tools characteristic of ordinary speech served as the main methodological tool for the writer.

Word usage is one of the important factors determining the artistic skill of a writer. However, the process of word usage involves various situations related to the word and its meanings. After all, many features of word usage are based on subtleties of meaning, using several words expressing the same concept, using the possibilities of words to create an image, using words in figurative meanings, and the writer chooses the situation of using words according to the content of his work. In our opinion, the elements of simple colloquial speech prevail in the formation of the artistic language of M.M.Dost's works.

In the linguistic analysis of the language of M.M. Dost's works, linguistics has relied on the traditions of the study of the language features of fiction. In addition, attention was paid to the textual structure of his works. The reason for this is that the textual structure of M.M.Dost's works, in which the speech of the author and the character is mixed, the speech of the characters is expressed in the way of thinking about the events and things in imagination, is the unique style of this writer. When studying a work of art from a lexical point of view, checking the words found in the work of art from the structural point of view, as well as explaining the function of words in the speech process, is the main factor of embodying the language of the work. It is known that, along with the tools typical for artistic speech, vocabulary tools that are not typical for artistic speech are also used in an artistic work. Revealing the functions of these tools in the text process is one of the tasks before researchers of this type.

The linguopoetics of synonyms in the writer's works

Synonyms are important lexical units that show the individual characteristics of the writer in the use of words. The role of synonyms in the process of artistic speech is determined by the fact that they express the concept at different levels. Because the words in the synonymous line can be expressed in different levels of the concept symbol, they can be distinguished from each other according to their emotional coloring. [50]These features allow for colorful expression of ideas in an artistic work.

The abundance of synonyms appropriately used in the work of art indicates the richness of the language of the work. After all, synonyms differ from other words in that they express not the same concept, but different levels of the same concept. Therefore, the more colorful the synonyms in the work, the more attractive the language of the work. The correct use of synonyms allows the writer to clarify the idea correctly and expressively, and prevents boring word repetition.

Any artistic work is primarily characterized by a wealth of synonyms. Because each of the synonyms has its own nuances of meaning, and they are used in a specific situation, according to the direction of the speech. There are texts in which the word used in it cannot be completely replaced by another synonym. This situation is one of the general characteristics of words, and it is more vividly embodied in synonyms. In the works of Murad Muhammad Dost, one can observe a particular uniqueness in the use of synonyms. In the works of the writer, there are many cases where the dialectal synonym of the word in the literary language is used, and in such usage, synonyms can show subtle meaning. For example,

---

[50]Hojiev A. An explanatory dictionary of synonyms of the Uzbek language. - Tashkent: Teacher, 1974. - B. 4.

on the contrary. It's as if there is a special filter in your throat that catches more lively words. The turnips will pass. *You can't speak more simply* ("Lolazor") is *the soul of the sentence* and *simple* words are synonyms. John's word has a coloring typical of oral speech. The concept of *"unspeakable words"* is expressed by the word "Jonnokh", while the meaning of "you don't say what's in your heart" is expressed by the word "Sajr".

In fact, the meaning of these synonyms expressing the concept of *"simple"* in this text is not a synonymous meaning, but a poetic meaning.

The synonym of the word "sodda " is used in order to emphasize the idea expressed in the text... *The times we were born in are different, and people are also different, and* in the sentence "Lolazor" ("Lolazor"), another synonym of this word *is* used.

In the work, the writer not only effectively used the synonyms specific to the language, but also created textual synonyms for the words. The use of such individual synonyms is achieved as a result of using the word in a figurative sense without departing from its original meaning.

fat means that the subject has more than a certain sign. For example, *Okhrik cannot claim, he is afraid, he has only a fat wallet* ("Lolazor"). Accordingly, this word is synonymous with the word *many* . The writer skillfully used the subtle meaning of the word "fat " in the meaning of *"a lot of money" and used the word "fat" (wallet)* to ensure his individual style. This situation shows that synonyms have special characteristics in the process of expressing meaning and that creators can provide diversity of the language of the work as a result of their effective use.

the writer uses the combination of *dark wallet* as a synonym for a fat wallet in the meaning of *"a lot of money"*, he uses the combination of empty wallet to express the opposite meaning . As a result, the synonyms *" fat wallet "* and *"dark wallet "* which means " a lot of money " indicate the writer's creativity. For example, *make the Wallet lighter, it may be necessary. You will get a marble stone for your brother's grave. My wallet was empty, fortunately, he put it in my pocket as he had some for the clothes of his wife and grandchildren.* ("Lolazor"). It can be observed that the words *"fat", "dark"* and *"puch"* are disconnected from the denotative meaning they usually express in these texts. The existence of the scheme of expressing the abundance, excess, lack of existing symbols in the meaning of these words was the basis for its use by the writer in the sense of *"a lot or a little money"* . The association between the use of the word fat mainly for domesticated animals and its relation to the fullness of the body and the appearance of a purse full of money suggests that there is an artistic expression in this usage. Or, it is logical to compare the words *"tok* " and " *puch* " with the words "tok" and "puch" being full and small compared to grain. It can be seen that the word *"fat" is used as a synonym for the word " thick"* in the author's work , and the concept of *"plurality" is* also expressed in it : *Many years have passed. Yakhaboev was distracted by a fatter work and almost forgot* about Qurbanoy ("Lolazor") the composition of *the work* expressed the concept of *"plurality"* in the sense of *"a large-scale work"* .

The important features of synonyms are the clarity and brightness of the thought expressed through them. For example, *even though we were simple, we laughed when we heard it, or rather, I laughed myself. And Oshna was smiling* ("Lolazor"). The words *laughed* and *smiled, which* generally express the same concept in the text, express different levels of the situation, so such expressions create great speech opportunities for the writer. The use of synonyms in accordance with the purpose serves to express a subtle meaning, can clearly embody the clarity of the image, fully reveal the psyche of the characters, as well as the attitude of a person to others, the uplifting and solemnity of the speech. For example, in the novel "Lolazor", the sentence that begins *with the words "It is more difficult to express the language or the style of tazarru" is from the speech of the hero of the novel, the writer Saidkul.* Therefore, in this sentence, high spirit, solemnity prevails. And the end of the sentence is completed as follows. *The truth is that even if we end lazy words at this place and draw a couple of hotter scenes on this oil, if we go closer to the main goal and events... The lazy* words used in this sentence , *hotter scenes* , lexical tools such as *drawing* are the basis for vividly embodying the idea that we want to express. The writer used the word lofty, solemn, lazy *words for words that are difficult for others to understand, and the word "hot"* for simple scenes , and created a new term for these concepts, specific to his artistic work. The use of a *closer synonym* of the word *"near"* has increased the rhetorical euphemism.

One of the main issues of the analysis of the artistic text is to determine the means of speech that play an important role in the creation of artistic expressiveness and imagery, and to reveal to what extent they match the content and essence of the speech process. Because the language tools do not remain the main material of the artistic work, but in the course of the development of the artistic language, they expand in terms of quality and acquire subtleties of meaning. As a result, with the help of such tools, the variety of artistic speech is created. The polishing of artistic speech and enrichment with artistic paints is connected with the development of fiction.

As the language of the work of art appears as an example of the art of words, it is provided on the basis of the variety of speech tools, the expression of different meanings of words, as well as the diversity of levels of expression of the meaning of the word. As a result of the expression of artistic figurative thought by means of speech, the colorfulness of the work of art is enhanced and its aesthetic impact is ensured. Synonyms are an important source of artistic creativity for the writer. Emotional-expressiveness increases especially when meaningful words characteristic of different forms of speech are used in the artistic text. For example: *The son of a real peasant, his demeanor also suits him. But you can't blame him for his cunning, he has a big farm, and you need to be a little cunning fox to manage such a big farm. - Well, I'm left alone! - exclaimed Yakhaboev. - It's a lie, you can tell from the way it's spoken, it's a stain* ("Lolazor"). The words *"quv", "sly", "duguli"* in the text are synonymous, " *quv*" is characteristic of oral speech, " *ayar* " is universal, and *"duguli"* is characteristic of archaic-book speech. Although these words convey the same meaning of *"cunning"* , each word has its own additional meaning. Consequently, the word *sly* has a negative connotation, and it can be observed that the negative connotation is weakened in the word *kuvligi* , which expresses this meaning, and the word *doguli* is used in a positive sense, meaning *"to caress"*.

The skillful use of synonyms ensures that synonyms play an important role in artistic texts and become a means of providing speech variety. Synonyms are a wealth of speech and are characterized by the fact that they express different levels of the same concept. The concept represented by the words in the series of synonyms creates the basis for the formation of artistic meaning. For example, *I could not reject Yakshoboev's words. Besides, I have* a bad *defect , I want to show my garden and boast* about it . *The word "guilt* " means an act against the established rules, and the word " *deficiency"* means a low level of compliance with the established rules.

It seems that the negative connotation is strong in both senses of the word. Therefore, the writer uses the word *kusur , which expresses a positive attitude to the above words, to express a habit that is not considered too blameworthy (that is, boasting about the garden)* . Because each synonymous expression has a subtle meaning and a stylistic color. The presence of subtleties of meaning in synonymous words is one of the important factors in the formation of artistic meaning. After all, the artistic meaning expressed by the synonym of *defect is to show that the speaker is the owner of a certain habit by expressing his innocence.*

Synonyms, along with expressing meaning, also serve as a stylistic tool in the text. For example, *he said something like, "Don't worry, I'm not a honey, God forbid I become a soft broom* ." The synonym of the word *"spoke"* in the sentence ("Lolazor") is distinguished by its artistic coloring and gives an artistic spirit to the text, while *the* simultaneous use of the synonyms " *asal"* and *"bal"* served to strengthen the intellectual emphasis.

Synonyms are lexical devices that are often used in speech in relation to other words and create various stylistic possibilities. That's why in literary texts, it can be observed that there are many non-literary synonyms of this or that word, and they fulfill different stylistic tasks: I am *afraid that they will threaten me, but they are extending me the first of friendship. I was happy. I had a lot of suspicion to make a fool out of myself...* ("Lolazor"). In this sentence , the synonyms of the word "doq" are used . The use of these words, along with the expression of the speaker's own speech, also ensured the solemnity of the artistic text.

One of the most important features of synonyms is that one of the words in the synonymous line belongs to a certain type of speech. Observing the works of Murad Muhammad Dost shows that in his work, synonyms characteristic of oral speech are used a lot and serve to create the characteristic of a certain place, the individual speech of characters. *"You are an idol," praised Yakhaboev. "You're still a great scholar-politician ."* This sentence is stylistically typical of simple colloquial speech. It is the speech of an uneducated teenager who has just left the village. Therefore, in the speech of an uneducated village teenager, the writer uses the common colloquial synonym of the word *miyang (head) , mainang, abbreviated idol of the whole word* , and many variants of the word *бок* , and while showing his unique speech, he also ensures textual simplicity in the text.

The use of words in artistic texts is based on the specific characteristics of the artistic text. As the main function of the artistic text is to be impressive, of course, it uses a lot of tools that organize the impressiveness and ensure the lexical uniqueness of the artistic style. Within the scope of synonyms, artistically colored forms of synonyms, which are characteristic for book speech, are distinguished by their speech stratification. Therefore, to explain , *express (saying), bright (exact), detailed (full), comprehensive (thorough), in writer works,* it can be observed that it is widely used and organizes artistic painting. After all, in artistic speech, every word can become an artistic tool in connection with the writer's skill of using words. This situation is more obvious when the words of the same synonymous line are used in the same place in a certain text. *Yakhaboev had a great appetite. Osno did his usual business. When he was full of joy, he took two or three bites, and then he turned away and sat looking with pleasure at his friend's food. Yakhaboev cleaned the food by wiping it with his fingers, smearing it with bread, and slowly spoke to his friend.* ("Lolazor"). In this sentence, synonyms such as " *to eat"* , *"to pinch", "to eat", "to clean" and "to clean" are used.* As a result of the use of these synonyms, first of all, boring repetition of the same word in the text was avoided. Also, each word has acquired its own meaning and stylistic coloring.

For example, if the word "*pinch*" expresses a lower than normal level of the concept of *"emoq"*, the word "*satisfy*" *expresses a positive attitude.* means *"to eat without leaving food"*. *The word to be cleaned is also used* as a synonym for this word. This word also has the concept of *"eating the food completely"*, *and this meaning is unique to this text.* In another text, *clean* may not be synonymous with these words. Accordingly, this word is synonymous with the synonymous line of *emaq*.

It should be noted that there are many tools that organize the figurative-artistic nature of the artistic text. It is known that the word possibilities of the language of fiction are limitless. Just as the words typical for all forms of universal lexical layers are effectively used in it, in the process of creating an artistic image, words typical for all speech styles can be used in a wide range. As the word is widely used in its literal and figurative meanings in the literary literature, it is possible to observe the general condition characteristic of the language of artistic works in the use of synonyms, word variants, and the use of various word forms and expressions. If the words are widely and freely used as in the language of fiction and perform a methodological function, then the free use of language tools at this level is one of the important features of fiction. After all, the creation of a number of words is directly related to the artistic text, which leads to the enrichment of the number of meaningful words in the language. The word *"hundred"* , which is often used in the works of Murad Muhammad Dost, is one such word. In fact, it can be seen that the word "*face* " which means *"to look"* is used in the writer's works not only in the sense of "looking" but in the sense *of the face falling on the face* . In this sense, this word is the subtle expression of the concept of "look" in the writer's works, the creation of a new meaning. *Then, when Halim forgot you completely, and when he was sitting in the car, Oshno turned to me and I spoke louder, Comrade Yakhasboev, now you will not be ashamed of this oil ("Lolazor"), I cry not for my belly, but for my value, my* boy *! - says Mrs. Muhsina, turning to Ollayor.* The word " *face"* used in the sentences ("Lolazor") expresses the meaning of *looking at the face* . In the word *look* , this meaning has a general expression.

"When you give money, you should look the person in the eye," said the old man. *"You didn't look?"* ("Return to Galatepa"). Or, the same meaning is generally expressed in the word *бокмок* , which is used as a synonym for the words given to express this concept . *He looked again at the yellow hills, he looked at the village panting in the depths of a small oasis, but he did not feel the old sorrow in his heart.* ("Lolazor"). The meaning of the word in the text depends on the creator's perception and skill in using words. The given synonyms can express other meanings instead. For example, *it's not a joke, who are you, the elder Raim's campaign... It is not good to sit in*

a dispute with a person who has put Galatepa in his mouth for fifty years. In the sentence ("Returning to Galatepa"), the word *directed* is not used in its original meaning, but in a metaphorical sense, expressing the concept of *"getting word of mouth among the people"*.

If synonyms are used to rank a sign in the meaning of a word or to express different aspects of a concept, it provides gloss and variety of speech. The word *moralamaq*, which means *"to look"*, is also characteristic in this respect: *He sat silently. When the "ambassador" has finished placing the things he brought, he goes to this side.* In the phrase "Lolazor", this word means *"look without noticing", "secret look"*.

If the synonymous words used in the speech express the same meaning and do not differ in terms of emotional coloring, they perform the function of expressing the meaning in new forms and provide diversity of the speech in terms of form. Such use of words avoids repetition of the same word and avoids boring, dense speech. - *Your way of thinking is more lively, Tashpolat, - said Samad. - If you think more simply, the words soulful* and *simple* in the sentence comrade ("Return to Galatepa") express the same meaning at the same level. One of the words is typical for ordinary speech and the other for the literary language, the fact that the words are used in their place in the text creates a speech tone and attractiveness, although replacing these words in the text does not affect the content of the expression, it leads to the loss of the tone.

Murad Muhammad Dost does not forget to ensure fluency and attractiveness of speech when using synonyms or when using a word as a synonym for another word. The use of the word " *spoken* " in the sense of "to speak" is characteristic in this respect.

Mrs. Muhsina woke up, looked at her husband with astonishment, smiled, and then, as if nothing had happened, as if she was going out the door and talking about what she had seen on the street, she spoke excitedly:

– Although we were young, we spared no one in terms of faith. This text is a text that demonstrates the selection of synonyms. The words andak *, bogdi, iljaydi , which* appear in it, have their own synonyms in the language, the word *iljaydi* differs from its synonyms in terms of expression, there is no difference in meaning in other words, but if these words are replaced by other synonyms in the text, it leads to a violation of speech fluency. This case indicates that these words are used interchangeably and are appropriate words for this discourse. A similar situation can be observed in the use of the word " *to speak"* . *The word said* can be used instead of this word . The writer deliberately uses the word *spoken* . Because this word differs from the word *dedi in that it expresses an incomplete thought, the word dedi* is mainly used to express a completed

thought. By the word *spoken* , the writer means to express an idea that has not yet been said and needs to be said. In this respect, this word can also be called a new word according to its meaning. The presence of the meaning of the *word sozli , which* is used as a synonym for this word , to report an event, shows that both are separate, independent words.

When using a certain word's meaning in a speech, the writer pays special attention to its compatibility with the text and its effect on the emotional coloring of the text. For example, *in general, women have a lot of meaningless chores, which they do not out of sincere devotion or need, but only to emphasize the merits of men* . given "The word work is mainly used in casual conversation and in the language of adults, and it is also used mainly for personal work and household chores [51]. " The difference in meaning between the words work and work is that they express broad and narrow concepts, and the word work has the meaning of "small, insignificant work". The word work is used because the text that the writer wants to express is thinking about the same work. This word is suitable for this speech and has linguopoetic value as it clearly expresses the thought to be expressed.

The writer also pays special attention to the appropriateness in terms of content when using meaningful

---

[51]Hojiev A. An explanatory dictionary of synonyms of the Uzbek language. - Tashkent: Teacher, 1974. - B. 111.

words in a certain speech process. For example, *I feel that this country is very wide, this country has many valleys, the mountains surrounding its valleys, and the villages that can be seen darkening in the heart of the mountains are* innumerable. , the mountains are also countless, it is difficult to express this concept through the word "many", therefore, the word "very" is used before the word, bringing the words closer to each other in terms of content, and providing intellectual balance to the speech.

Murad Muhammed Dost creates synonymous relations using the polysemy of words. For example, the word rare is a word that expresses the concept of "scarcity" in relation to the germination of a grain crop. Using this subtlety of meaning, the writer used this word as a synonym for the word "kam" to ensure the effectiveness of the intellectual expression. *When the time comes, the elder Raim will be lonely, the chiefs will no longer come to him, there are few people who ask for advice, he and his past, a couple of noisy old men... ("* Return to Galatepa"). In general, there is an artistry in the use of the word *rare* in relation to a person, a human action, because this word has created a new meaning based on the comparison of a state with another state. The following examples show that synonyms are used selectively in the writer's works according to the nature and direction of speech. *This is a very conditional border, an invisible border, but now I understand the necessity of crossing it. It is difficult for a stubborn, proud person to cross my threshold.* ("Lolazor"). The words *"dushvor "* and *"difficult"* in the quoted sentences are similar in meaning. The first sentence is solemn according to the style of speech, so the word "dushvor" characteristic of poetic style is used in it, while the word "difficult" is used in the second sentence because it is typical of a simple style.

The writer also made good use of the meaning of words and phrases in his works. The meaning of words and phrases, in our opinion, is worth a separate study on the example of the writer's works. At this point, we found it necessary to limit ourselves to giving some examples. In terms of the meaning of words and phrases, the writer made good use of the rich lexical possibilities of the national language and achieved to express an emotionally impressive idea. For example, *Imza has a habit of blowing his nose while smoking, which Hamraqul always interprets as a sigh, and he always smiles.* ("Resignation") The word *iljaymoq* does not mean laughing, but the presence of this state in lip movements. In the "Annotated dictionary of synonyms of the Uzbek language" it is explained that this word is used in the meanings of "to express laughter with lip movements, to laugh with a smile" [52].

---

[52] Hojiev A. Source indicated. - B. 97.

Murad Muhammad Dost was able to express this meaning by using the expression "the lips are tight" and he was able to ensure the artistic perfection of the text.

The poor man tried hard to be humble, to speak softly, but he couldn't do it, his lips tightened and he revealed his satisfaction ("Lolazor"). The expressiveness of expressions such as *stressing, trying hard, and expressing satisfaction* in this sentence is enhanced by the use of the expression *"puckered lips"*.

In general, the works of Murad Muhammad Dost embody all aspects of the Uzbek folk colloquial language, in which the writer tried to use synonyms appropriately.

A writer's skill in using broad vocabulary

In the linguistic study of a work of art, the examination of the words found in the work from the point of view of its composition, as well as the interpretation of the function of words in the speech process, are important factors in embodying the language of the work. It is known that in an artistic work, in addition to the tools typical for artistic speech, vocabulary tools that are not typical for artistic speech are used, and they show the artistic-aesthetic essence. Therefore, revealing the functions of lexical tools in the speech process, which are not characteristic of artistic speech, is one of the important issues for researchers of the language of artistic works. In linguistics, there are very few studies based on the speech style of the lexical units of the language of the artistic work. However, artistic texts lexically cover the tools specific to all styles of the language.

It should be noted that the words used in the works of art do not have the importance of being specific to any speech style, therefore, the skill of using words in this type of speech is determined by the function of the word in the speech process. After all, in artistic speech, the words that are typical for any type of speech become a tool for expressing an artistic-impressive thought as a result of the artist's skill in using words.

Prof. A.I.Efimov explains the lexical richness of the language of the artistic work by the use of words belonging to different lexical groups [53]. Accordingly, in the study of the language of an artistic work, taking into account all the linguistic tools in it, the analysis based on the function of the language tools becomes important in the study of the language features of the artistic work.

If we approach the study of Murad Muhammad Dost's works from this point of view, it can be seen that the author's works are lexically created on the basis of book words, widely used words and words related to oral speech.

---

[53] Efimov A.I. Stylistics of artistic speech. - M .: Education, 1961. - S. 206

Literary words are lexical units of the language dictionary that are used for literary speech and are divided into general and artistic-literary words according to the scope of use. Literary words are important vocabulary tools for an artistic work, they are used in order to ensure the elation and attractiveness of the speech, and to give artistic color to the speech. Literary words form a group of archaic and modern words from the point of view of literary language. Archaic words are words that are still in use today, mostly found in historical works. Modern artistic and literary words are words found in some types of speech, mainly for artistic speech.

If the works of Murad Muhammad Dost are analyzed in terms of the use of these vocabulary tools, it can be observed that the writer almost did not use obsolete words. However, every artist uses a certain amount of obsolete words. In the works of M.M. Dost , there are several archaisms such as *mukhtasar, mahdudlik, ghussa, sarkashlik, dorilfunun, gaddor, ghanim, sarkhushlik and* historical words such as *shura, madrasa, farsah, caravan, caravansaray, caravanbashi, chorik, saroybon, ulus* .

The cabinet did not arouse anger as before. Neither good nor bad, he thought. Fortunately, Elomonov's father was a shepherd and did not speak loudly to the nation. The obsolete words *ghussa* and *ulus* in the sentences ("Resignation") are used in the text as a nomema, the writer did not intend to use these words in any stylistic manner.

This situation can be explained as follows. The writer's works are devoted to modern topics, and events related to the past are hardly depicted in it. Therefore, the writer does not feel the need to use archaic and historical words in his works. It should be noted that the obsolete words found in the writer's works mainly performed the function of naming according to their stylistic features.

In one or two parts of the novel "Lolazor" by Murad Muhammad Dost, events specific to the past are described and historical words are used in these parts. For example, the words *machit and caravanserai in the phrase "machit" and "caravansaroy"* in the sentence *"they came to Ortakurgan, wandered around without acquaintances, and finally found a place in the caravanserai near the mosque"* are words that express the way of life of that time, and the text also expresses the meaning of naming.

The same situation can be observed in the use of literary and literary words, which are considered lexical tools defining the important features of artistic speech in the writer's works.

Therefore, in the works of the writer, literary speech *such as joy, feeling, feeling, quiet, moment, ocean, sadness, longing, bright, place, news, believe, strange, whole, sorrow, rain, heart, turn, silence, drunkenness, anger* although there are specific words, artistic and literary words are not active in terms of their use in the works of Murad Muhammad Dost, on the contrary, the writer's works are based on words typical of wide consumption and oral speech. The lexical uniqueness of the writer's works can be explained as follows. First, in the author's works, the story is mainly told in the language of the heroes of the work. The heroes of the work are mostly ordinary representatives of the people, literary and literary words are not specific units for their speech, therefore, words related to book speech are often used in the author's speech.

During the mentioned period, Oshno could feel the ringing. He didn't even care that his heart beat faster because of pride in his heart. In general, he was happy when Oshno called, but this last one... a call that can be heard from thousands of kilometers away, how many oceans and how many oceans... The words pride, pride, times, joy, sea, ocean in the sentence ("Lolazor") are characteristic of the book style. is used in the author's speech. Secondly, since the heroes of the writer's works are not representatives of a profession, words of profession and terms of the profession are very rare in the writer's work. Thirdly, the lexical coherence of all the writer's works is built on the basis of the national language, the expression of thoughts in simple and simple expressions leads to the conclusion that this method of using language tools is an individual style chosen by the writer.

Wide usage words make up an important part of the language vocabulary. Broad usage words are words that are widely used in everyday life and are understood by many people and are characterized by their methodological neutrality [54]. While thinking about the lexical layers of the Uzbek literary language, E. Begmatov rightly admitted that this lexical layer has not been studied [55].

In linguistics, the words used in everyday life and understood by everyone in this lexical layer [56] are called lexical units of the general language layer [57], lexicon in general use [58], lexicon with unlimited scope of use . [59] As a result of considering these lexical units as neutral words, researchers of artistic discourse have not paid much attention to studying the functions of these lexical tools in the process of artistic discourse. Therefore, in several studies devoted to the analysis of artistic speech, it can be seen that the speech functions of widely used words are analyzed. For example, S. Boboeva in the first chapter of her research on the topic "Lexical-stylistic

---

[54] Begmatov E. Lexical layers of the current Uzbek literary language. - Tashkent: Science, 1985. - B. 11.
[55] Begmatov E. This work. - B. 11
[56] Mirzaev M., Usmanov S., Rasulov I. Uzbek language. - Tashkent: Teacher, 1970. - B. 32.
[57] Tursunov U., Mukhtorov J., Rahmatullaev Sh. Modern Uzbek literary language. - Tashkent: Teacher, 1975. - B. 62.
[58] Shoabdurahmanov Sh., Askarova A., Hojiev A., Rasulov I., Doniyorov Kh. Modern Uzbek literary language. - Tashkent: Teacher, 1980. - B. 127.
[59] Lexicology of the Uzbek language. - Tashkent: Science, 1981. - B. 11 - 16.

features of Hamid Olimjon's poetry" analyzes the poet's use of popular words for stylistic purposes [60], while S. Tursunov studies the lexical features of the "Alpomish" epic, popular words are important tools that provide artistic speech, especially in folklore works. pays special attention to the fact [61]that B. Umurkulov in his monograph "Word in Literary Literature" interpreted these lexical units as important lexical units of artistic speech.

For example, common words in the process of artistic speech, firstly, combine words of all layers, and secondly, the degree of expression of meaning compared to words of other layers is wide and ambiguous [62]. Ambiguity in commonly used words is analyzed through examples showing that the word tag is used in 18 meanings, and the verb to put is used in 13 meanings [63]. The scientist came to the following conclusions based on the analysis of the function of common words in the process of artistic speech. "Common words form the main lexical layer of any artistic work. Commonly used words are the basis for the creation of a large number of visual tools found in

---

[60]Babayeva S. Lexico-stylistic features of Hamid Alimjan's poetry. Abstract ...diss. cand. philol. Sciences. - Tashkent: 1989. - P. 17.
[61]Tursunov S. Lexical features of the dastan "Alpamysh". - Tashkent: 1990. - P. 7.
[62]Umurkulov B. Word in fiction. - Tashkent: Science, 1993. - B. 59.
[63]Umurkulov B. Featured work. - B. 65 - 67.

artistic works, and they are also the basis for expressing figurative and impressive thoughts [64].

The works of Murad Muhammad Dost, which are studied as the object of this research, are a source that fully demonstrates the stylistic features of popular words.

Common words, like other lexical tools, are words that are actively used in all types of speech, and in works of art, these lexical units are mainly manifested through the speech of characters. Commonly used words are mainly used as a means of expressing meaning in the text, but they also have the characteristics of providing intellectual coloring, as well as the words of literary and literary meaning. Wide usage words are lexical units that are used several times more often than words from other layers in a work of art. For example, *I didn't say anything. Honestly, I hesitated for a while. A tendency to believe was born. But there is one more thing, I thought that if I am a slave like him, I have a warm soul, and it is not a cruel arrogance to take on someone else's struggle* ("Lolazor")

This text is a text with artistic expression and impact, and in terms of word usage, it mainly consists of broad usage words. Effectiveness in the text is based on skillful use of words in the process of expressing thoughts. The skillful use of words such as *indamadim, to believe, tendency, istihola, and pride*

---

[64]Umurkulov B. Featured work. - B. 72.

gave the text an artistic color. This text shows that the possibility of expressing an artistically colorful thought through the medium of widely used words in artistic speech is unlimited. After all, common words are one of the important lexical layers that provide speech effectiveness and form the basis of the vocabulary of an artistic work.

The function of common words in artistic discourse is one. Consequently, the lexical tools of this layer are lexical units characterized by the freedom of meaning expression, the wide range of usage in figurative meanings, and the features of polysemy compared to other words used in artistic texts.

An important feature of the literary text is that the words serve to provide the artistry. The place of widely used words in artistic speech is determined by the fact that they create artistry and impressiveness. From this point of view, it was observed that in organizing the artistic coloring of the language of Murad Muhammad Dost's works, in ensuring the effectiveness, the words of general consumption served as basic lexical units.

"Television," Mrs. Muhsina advised.

- If you put it higher, the voice of the crow will not be heard.

- What if the crows are in the mood? - said Yakhaboev more forcefully. - What if it is knocking in the heart?

– Let's make the breath hotter, daddy! ("Lolazor")

The cited text is also composed by means of widely used words, the use of the word *crow in the figurative* sense, the use of the phrase "to panic" as a result of the use of the phrase "to panic" as a result of the expression of the meaning of "restlessness, to be worried about something" ensured the richness of the text and led to the expression of an impressive idea. Also, as a result of the addition of the suffix *-roq* in the words louder, harder, hotter, these words can express a subtle meaning.

The second situation that gives artistic color to the text is the repetition of the thought. In the quoted passage, although the thought is not exactly repeated, there is a logical repetition. This situation is formed on the basis of the repeated use of the word heart, *what if it is in the heart, what if it is knocking in the heart? repetitions have strengthened the meaning of "concern"* that is meant to be expressed in essence.

This text analysis shows that in a work of art, words not only express meaning, but also serve to create a poetic image. The emergence of imagery and artistic effectiveness through words is manifested on the basis of the unity of form and content of the text, that is, if the content of a certain form corresponds to this form, and the word used in it also corresponds to the form and content, intellectual effectiveness is created. The writer Murad Mohammad Dost uses different ways of using words to adapt the word to form and content. Adding the suffix *-roq* to many words in the novel is one such method. *"Ours is worse," said Yakhaboev, then thought of a pain that seemed worse to him, and laughed inside. - There is a big spot in the lung.* The words in this position can be used without the *suffix -roq* and the meaning will not be affected. However, the writer chooses a form that expresses the content he wants to express with the help of this suffix, and this form shows that the writer was able to create his own style of expression. One of the important means of vividly embodying the language of the writer's works is the use of *many* adverbial words and their function of expressing subtle meaning. For example, *thanks to this booklet, my path was opened, I joined a similar, if not larger, line.*

Higher hills join flatter mountains. Jonuza Arab was a little more talkative and unassuming. ("Lolazor") These quoted texts show that the writer used many words with the suffix *-roq*, *assuming that they create certain stylistic possibilities.*

The main feature of artistic speech is the possibility to express in detail the character, inner world, changes in a person, various mental states, events, natural images, the place where the events described in the work took place. In this process, artistic speech shows the features of imagery and emotionality. Therefore, in order to enhance the aesthetic impact of the work, the writer in the artistic speech should use the phonetic and morphological features of the language, as well as visual means.

The skill of the writer is to choose the linguistic tools that ensure the text is at the level of artistic text requirements, and to be able to use it in a situation suitable for the speech process.

"To assess whether the use of words is at the level of art or not at the level of art, " writes prof. M. Yoldoshev, - first of all, it is necessary to clearly imagine the word, its meaning and the structure of this meaning. Of course, additional subtleties of meaning and differences in content that appear in connection with the use of the word can be realized through various image methods and tools [65].

The scientist continues his thought and shows the existence of such additional subtleties of meaning as a possibility of adding meaning to words. The fact that the writer Murad Mohammad Dost used the suffix *-roq in many places can be explained from this point of view.*

This adverb is used in addition to adjectives in the language. However, in the writer's works, it can be observed that it is used in conjunction with many verbs. For example, *He seemed to hit Gaybarov in the mouth. The young man looked at him less favorably* ("Return to Galatepa"), *although we have known each other for many years, I was still more in awe of him* ("Lolazor").

---

[65] Yoldoshev M. Basics of literary text and its linguopoetic analysis. - Tashkent: Science, 2007, - B.49.

In the quoted sentences, the suffix *-roq* is added to the words of the verb group, meaning that the action-state expressed by the meaning of the word is at a lower level than usual. In fact, the existence of this subtlety of meaning was the basis for the writer to express an impressive opinion.

Another means of determining the effectiveness of an artistic text is the creation of a new form of expression in the work. The creation of a new form of expression is determined by finding new forms of language tools and using them in accordance with speech, as well as by demonstrating the skill of using words in the use of words that already exist in the language. The novel "Lolazor" is a work that attracts attention with the creation of new forms of expression. The speech of each character in the work has its own form of expression. For example, *Yakhaboev was lying in bed. It's useless to talk, you can still move, all the organs are in place. Yakshoboev doesn't smile, he wanted to say, "You've raised my pain again."* It seems that these thoughts were said by Yakhaboev, but they were not said, but thought by Yakhaboev. In the work, especially in the depiction of events related to the life of Yakhaboev, his thoughts are expressed in many places and he organizes the originality of the style of the work.

In addition, thought-based texts, although the bulk of them are built on the basis of widely used words, have a significant emotional impact, even if they do not have pictorial means. Undoubtedly, this situation arose on the basis of the choice of the form of expression suitable for the content.

Like all the words in the language dictionary, in the work of Murad Muhammad Dost, the words of general consumption also played an important role in providing artistic coloring. These lexical tools were the basis for the creation of many visual tools, just as images and artistic painting were created with the help of common words.

One of the important features of buzzwords is their thematic diversity. Therefore, with the help of the words of this layer, there are names of actions and situations, names of things and events, expressions of human feelings and situations, expressions of relationships between people, names of human organs, in short, there are words with all the meanings necessary for the expression of human thoughts. This situation shows that the level of meaning expression of common words is unlimited, and in artistic works, words of this level primarily serve as a tool for expressing ideas.

However, the role of popular words in the process of artistic speech is not limited to this. This lexical layer is rich in synonyms and has the features of figurative expression. The words of this layer are particularly distinguished by their polysemy. In the works of the writer, there are many places where artistic coloring and impressiveness are organized based on the figurative use of popular words. For example, *is it any wonder that our swallows later turn into eagles and fly higher?! The words swallow and eagle* in the sentence express a figurative meaning. If the two young men who are going from the village to the city to study are leaving their home, the word "swallow" represents the fact that they will acquire knowledge and become experts in the future. In these sentences, the impact of the idea is enhanced on the basis of the transfer of the meaning of the word.

It can be observed in the following examples that intellectual richness is ensured based on the use of broad consumer words in figurative meanings: <u>vitamin</u> (*I can't get so many vitamins, - said Yakhasboev, embarrassed, you tell the owner first*) here the word *vitamin* is used in the sense of *"fruit"* . *To make a mustache* in the sense of *"pointing"* (*Khorshanbiev slowly "whiskered" the film guy while Kakhshoboev was sitting with his head bowed, "get out, they won't welcome you"*). The meaning of " many roads *traveled* " with the words " *Bells* rang *, the camels neighed, the passengers swayed, the Ortakaurgon road kept getting more and more" "Nokboron"* , the meaning of *"water running from my nose " is given* by means of the words (*...putting on a more spacious jacket, suffering and sweating in the hope of changing my waist from dol to alif, I came to the meeting building with a spring running from my nose*) is widely used by the writer. it shows that he skillfully used the features of figurative expression of his words. It is worth noting that the words *"vitamin", "nokboron"* and *"cut to cut"* in the given examples are characteristic of the writer's individual style.

The writer's works show how wide the level of meaning expression of words in the language is by skillfully using the polysemous properties of common words. For example, in the novel, the original meaning of the word *"to look" is expressed by the word "look" (* Then *I looked, Yakhasboev pulled away sadly*), the meaning of *"direction"* (*Now I was walking towards the train station, when two acquaintances came out from inside*), *"the meaning of having a good relationship" "* (*Both of them are very thick, they look at each other while sitting and standing*), in the sense of *"seeing"* (*When moviegoers come and look, their director is opening twenty boxes of unopened film, screwing it up, and measuring it like gas with a gas stick in his hand*), as well as *" take away" (-My mother-in-law looks after. After the widow doesn't hear from handsome old men like you... she looks after her grandchildren, whatever she does*) is also observed.

To leave something in the original meaning of the word " stay" to someone (*We would leave the world behind, my dear, we will leave it to them!*), *"to remember"* (*Iskander's conquests in the war would only be a memory*) , *"to be silent"* (*Kakhsboev took the hand of Mrs. Muhsina, pressed his lips. They remained silent*), *"to be ashamed"* (*Tell me, don't hide it, if I don't fit in your day at this time, then what will I have to do*) shows the existence of a number of subtle meaning expression possibilities with this word. A skillful use of this kind of subtlety of meaning in common words can be seen in the usage of the following words. For example, the word ` `open'`', except for its original dictionary meaning, is *"fresh air"* (*as soon as they went out into the open air, Gaybarov felt love in his heart, his chest seemed to burst* "Return to Galatepa"), *"cloudless, good day"* (*-The air is clear. -He travels here every day it is not necessary to shave*), *"not to speak openly"* (*he can't openly make allegations, he is afraid, I have only a fat wallet.* "Lolazor") *"to talk freely"* (*-After becoming friends...-said Gaybarov. -What will you do if you want to talk more openly?. ..* "Return to Galatepa") is used to express the meaning of the term, which shows the polysemy of the common words.

The writer's skill in using the tools of oral speech

Oral speech tools are vocabulary tools used for the oral form of speech, and A.V. Kalinin admits that these language tools are used in oral forms of speech, but not in written form. therefore, he emphasizes that the artistic work includes stylistically neutral, colloquial, as well as high-style words [66].

A large part of the vocabulary of artistic texts is made up of oral speech tools. The use of oral speech tools in artistic texts

---

[66] Kalinin A.V. Lexicon of the Russian language. - M.: Moscow University, 1978. - S. 175.

can be explained as follows. Firstly, these means of speech have a wide possibility of providing imagery and impressiveness, and secondly, the means of oral speech are colorful in terms of emotional-expressiveness and differ from their neutral synonyms with a very strong sign-level in the meaning of the word. This situation is useful for expressing the thought in all its subtlety. Thirdly, the life of ordinary people is depicted in the work of art. Since the characters in it are representatives of the common people, it is natural that in their speech they use vocabulary tools that are typical for the common colloquial speech of the people.

Linguist B. Orinboev distinguishes three different elements in the forms of colloquial speech taken from works of art.

1. Lexical and grammatical elements that correspond to the norms of the literary language.

2. Word forms and grammatical forms that express the characteristics of spoken language and pronunciation.

3. Dialectism and elements of local dialect.

The scientist shows that the use of the second and third of these language tools found in the speech of the characters of the work is related to the skill of the writer, they are used in order to ensure the uniqueness of the speech of the hero [67]. The researcher notes the presence of special emotional-figurative words in the lexicon of colloquial speech, rich in strong emotional and imagery [68]. The means of oral speech are the second form of the elements of colloquial speech in the classification of B. Orinboev, and are distinguished from other means of colloquial speech by their non-availability in general use, their individuality and emotional coloring. The issues of the role of oral speech tools in artistic speech have not been sufficiently analyzed in Uzbek linguistics. Some sources comment on the role of the means of oral speech in artistic speech. Prof. S. Karimov emphasizes that the use of dialecticisms characteristic of oral speech style in artistic works originates from the individualization of characters' speech, giving local color, fulfilling an aesthetic task [69].

B.Umurkulov explains that the means of oral speech are rich sources of the language of artistic works and that they are often used in artistic texts as follows. "Oral speech is rich in figurative, emotional-expressive means, in this respect it corresponds to the essence of the language of fiction, and the means of oral speech serve to express an artistic-impressive

---

[67] Orinboev B. Problems of Uzbek language colloquial speech syntax. - Tashkent: Science, 1974, - B. 8 - 9.
[68] Orinboev B. Featured work. - B. 16.
[69] Karimov S. Artistic style of the Uzbek language. - Samarkand: Zarafshan, 1992, - B. 122.

thought in this type of speech. [70]" B. Umurkulov explains the use of words characteristic of different forms of speech in artistic speech by the fact that the language of fiction literature is a form of the folk language reflected in an artistic work and has an artistic color. In his opinion, the emotional-expressiveness and expressiveness of words characteristic of oral speech do not lose their power even when used in artistic speech. Therefore, the means of oral speech are a component of the lexicon of artistic speech [71].

While thinking about the role of oral speech tools in artistic speech, R. Normurodov shows that the characters of the artistic work belong to different classes, and the signs of belonging to each social group are reflected through the lexical tools specific to oral speech [72].

Literary critic G.Imomova, while thinking about the language of an artistic work, emphasizes that the language of an artistic work requires compatibility of form and content, obeys the laws of individualization, and covers all forms of literary language and lively conversational language with its artistic aesthetic quality [73].

---

[70] Umurkulov B. Word in fiction. - Tashkent: Science, 1993. - B. 106.
[71] Umurkulov B. Featured work. - B. 106 - 107.
[72] Normurodov R. Artistic skills of Shukur Kholmirzaev. - Tashkent: 2003. - B. 82.
[73] Imamova G. Nationalism and artistic speech. - Tashkent, 2004. - B. 28.

The mentioned points show that there are strong grounds for the use of oral speech tools in artistic speech. Therefore, it performs many tasks such as embellishing the speech, bringing the language of the writer's works closer to the vernacular, ensuring its simplicity, and lexically enriching the language of the work, and these features also ensure the active use of these tools in artistic speech. Since the heroes of the work of art are representatives of the common people, it is natural for their speech to use lexical tools typical of the common colloquial speech of the people. An important aspect that shows the essence of artistic speech is that it uses vocabulary tools specific to different speech styles, as well as different forms of language, and creates methodological possibilities. In this sense, the essence of the means of oral speech is determined by ensuring methodicality in artistic speech.

Since the aesthetic impact and expressiveness of the speech is an important sign of the artistic speech, vocabulary units rich in impressive and expressive means are selected and used in order to create various stylistic possibilities for this form of speech. Means of oral speech are also distinguished from other lexical units in this respect. Because the means of oral speech are distinguished by their emotional-expressive coloring even outside the text, and in the text this situation is even more exaggerated. For example, *if a blind person doesn't like my appearance, it's obvious that you don't like it, - said Yakhasboev with a laugh* . The word *blind* in the text is typical of speech. This word is characterized by the fact that it is used in a figurative sense. After all, a blind person cannot see a person's appearance, and after not seeing, the concept of whether or not he likes remains abstract. It seems that this word was used not in the sense of *"blind"* , *but in the sense of "indifferent, insightless person"* and based on this meaning provided emotional-expressiveness.

Murad Muhammad Dost's works are rich in oral speech tools, in which there are many vocabulary units specific to oral speech, which are used based on the repetition of words in connection with the individual style of the writer.

You used to see me on television - don't think that he's coming and sticking around now, domlajon ("Lolazor"). *Put your Ashur-Pashur, Wednesday child, find out for yourself* ("Lolazor") *TV-television,* based on the use of the second part of the words Ashur-Pashur, provided specificity to oral speech.

By the use of words in this way in the work, it is expressed that the hero is a representative of the common people, and thus the simplicity of the language of the work and its closeness to the language of the people is ensured.

The kairagoch-payragogoch used in the play (*Where, - said Yakhasboev, shrugged his shoulders. - It would be good if we were lucky enough to be a krajagoch-payragogoch. Lokin-pokin (Your trust is very great! - exclaimed Kulak). - There is no need for lokin-pokin. Markes - The use of a word such as Parkes (...the marques-parkes who wrote those jungle-selvas are better than us!* "Lolazor") is used in the case of adaptation to oral speech by reduplication in the second part of the word.

The means of oral speech are diverse in terms of content. It contains words typical of oral literary speech, words typical of ordinary speech, words typical of rough speech, and the use of words in dialectal forms also ensures belonging to oral speech. One of the important features of these means of speech is the strong emotional coloring in words, therefore, strong expression of feelings is provided with the help of such words. For example, if *Anovi, megajin, manjalaki, follows the moustached hezalak called husband, becomes cultured and enters the house from which he was divorced again!* The sentence ("Lolazor") consists mainly of words typical of oral speech. Words such as *megajin, manjalaqi, hezalak, kultunyi are used to express the speaker's hatred.* These words are rude means of speech, and in their meaning *"insult", "swear"* has a strong meaning, therefore, these lexical means are used to express *"hatred"* .

Through the means of speech used in this text, it can be seen that the words characteristic of speech perform the function of naming and create stylistic possibilities in the text. Such features are especially strongly manifested in the means of oral speech, which are characteristic of rude speech. *Meowing like a cat* in the play *(...What about those who meowed like a cat?..*

True, later the fire in Muhsina's heart died out), a pig in the field (He doesn't know that Yakhasboev, who is a pig in your eyes , was very *clean at that time)* Lexical tools such as *(...does that ugly bastard still read other people's books after his death ?)* are tools that can vividly embody their skills.

The following lexical tools used in the writer's works, which are distinguished by different subtleties of meaning, also have their own subtleties of meaning and are distinguished by the characteristic of emotional-expressive coloring. For example, *in the voice of Mamashokirov, you could feel the pain. Elomonov's anger increases, I can't get out with one, not three, the other two are fine. As* in the sentence ("Resignation") , *I can't get out, honest* words are characteristic of oral speech. If the words *andak and durost* are used in a denotative sense, they mean that the hero of the work is a representative of the common people, and the word " *I can't agree* " *is used to express the "inability to agree" characteristic of oral speech.* the expression of its meaning indicates that these tools are an important lexical unit in the process of artistic speech. *...Haybatulla teacher, Landavur teacher Haibatulla, Anoyi, Anqov, Azbaroi would not be equal to thugs if the salt did not dry up! If the words landavur, anoyi, and anqov in* the sentence ("Lolazor") express the high level of the meaning of *"empty", "not being able to do anything",* he added words like *"don't worry, I'm not a honey bee myself, God forbid I become a soft* *broom"* ("Lolazor") is expressed in a strong emotional- *painting* sense by means of a *soft broom* phrase in the sentence.

While thinking about the richness of the emotional-expressive means of the language of a work of art, B. Umurkulov said that the emotional-expressive means typical of oral speech in fiction perform the task of characterizing the characters, expressing the writer's attitude and forming positive or negative attitudes towards the character in the reader, accordingly, emphasizes that the language of fiction cannot be imagined without emotional-expressive means of oral speech [74]. Emotional-coloring in many means of oral speech is related to the expression of meaning at different levels. Also, the fact that a certain word expressing a meaning found in oral speech is not present in other types of speech, including general speech, shows that oral speech is a source of diversity in the language. For example, *Wednesday is a great guy, he freezes his work, the notary has a doctor next to him...* The fact that the word *freezes* in the sentence ("Lolazor") does not exist in the literary language and in general usage indicates that it is a means of oral speech. This word, which is mainly used in ordinary speech and has moved to artistic speech, is characterized by the fact that it expresses the meaning of *"doing something above the norm"* . Most of the means of oral speech have emotional-

---

[74]Umurkulov B. Word in fiction. Tashkent: Science, 1993. - B. 108.

expressiveness on the basis of their differences from their counterparts in the language, and are adapted to be used in artistic speech embodying this characteristic. In the works of the writer Murad Mohammad Dost, there are many oral speech tools that have the characteristics of expressing a subtle meaning. For example, *Yakshoboev brewed soup and put on the table the treats brought by the elder and our own. we reached and made the gurung bloom. Here's the thing, Comrade Yakhaboev, we will seriously look into this matter: You, keep your heart full and let your creativity flourish. To flourish* in the conjunctions of the *phrase* "Lolazor". the word expresses the meaning of performing a certain action at a high level. One of the important aspects of the means of oral speech is that it acquires a formative characteristic with a means of language. The word *gullatmaq* in the given example also exists in the literary language and differs from its counterpart in oral speech in terms of expression. The same situation can be observed in *the* following sentence . ...*on the one hand, the artist people are singing songs in Farghan, Khorezm, and Fuzili.* ("Lolazor"). The word *olıpı* in this text is *"to get"* not the meaning, *"the song is good* **express the meaning of** *"to say"* and acquired an emotional-expressive character according to its expression. Emotional-painting becomes stronger in figurative words. Means of oral speech expressing a new meaning based on polysemy, metaphorical meaning in literary texts are important sources of lexical enrichment of artistic speech. Because these tools have strong features of polysemy, figurative expression. In the works of the writer, there are many cases of verbal speech tools that express several meanings and are used figuratively. It is known that if language means expresses a new meaning, it becomes a new word and has the feature of providing speech diversity. For example, *no matter what happens, Pirimkul's brother, Salamat's bride, is not a stranger. Here, they went to the vessel and came themselves, they are asking for consent. It's good, after all, it's good that you have a vein.* The verb vein in the sentence ("Mustafa") is characteristic in this respect. According to the expression of the meaning of *brothers*, this word enriched the language and artistic speech from a lexical point of view, and created a diversity of speech. The fact that there are several lexical tools that serve to express a certain meaning is the richness of the language, especially in artistic speech. This situation is evident on the basis of the word's polysemy and when it is used in figurative senses. For example, the word *landing* is used in the common language to refer to the fact that birds have completed their flight. In the writer's work, it is observed that it is used in different meanings related to this meaning, and according to these expressions, the non-existence of this word in the literary language shows that it is characteristic of oral speech. *Tolkinov put his right hand on the steering wheel and left his hat on the seat. Yargag scratched his* head, then put his hat on his head. In the sentence ("Resignation"), the word *kondirdi* means *"to put down"*, *Izlab came and landed at the teahouse in the market.* In the sentence ("Return to Galatepa") it is used in the sense of *"settled"*.

Figurative meaning is also one of the important features of the means of oral speech. In the works of the writer Murad Muhammad Dost, there are many figurative language tools. For example, *"Your speech is so cold," he said. - My brother still has a long day.* The word *cold* in the sentence ("Mustafa") is *"a bad word", many days* in the meaning of *"lives a lot"* created artistic coloring in the text. It can also be observed in the following examples that oral speech tools provide richness based on figurative expression. <u>He talked about it </u>(*It's not a joke, who are you, Raim the elder's campaign... It's not good to sit in a dispute with someone who has been talking about Galatepa for fifty years.* "Return to Galatepa"), <u>he avoided the conversation </u>(*Maybe there were some misunderstandings that I didn't know about, and the conversation escaped between them, <u>but</u> they did n't reveal <u>such </u>things . You walk carelessly, but one day you see that you are full, you can't help but let your heart <u>go</u>* . in the sense of (*I now understand whose husband I plowed, now, when I am no longer fit to plow.* "Resignation"), <u>to sing </u>in the sense of *"to speak"* (*- I sing, - said the old woman. - What are you beating?* "Mustafa"), in the sense of *"life"* <u>with open</u>

123

eyes (*With his father Everything was fine when his mother's eyes were open.* "Mustafa").

One of the characteristics of the means of oral speech is the availability of synonyms of many lexical units in the literary language. For example, *a good* word in literary language *right, want* of the word forms typical of oral speech, such as *tusab, are found in the writer's works as means of characterizing the characters' speech.* For example, *it was good that Bugun Ibodulla Makhsum came, Elomonov was walking around the village without him.* ("Resignation"). *A flower* that has a synonym in the literary language in the writer's works (simple), *neat* (good), *when* (in my opinion), *not so much* (nothing, nothing), *etc* (a little), *right* (good), *siyak* (appearance), *sink* (sit down), *jo'n* (simple), *joyali* (proper) and many other means of speech were used to create speech uniqueness.

Means of oral speech are different - district. From the point of view of stylistic coloring, relation to literary language, A.V. Kalinin divided the tools of oral speech into colloquial lexicon and ordinary colloquial (prostorechnuyu) lexicon, and noted that the colloquial lexicon is neutral in relation to other types of oral speech, and the ordinary colloquial lexicon is outside the norms of the literary language as their different aspects. shows [75].

---

[75] Kalinin A.V. Featured work. - B. 157-159.

B. Umurkulov also divides the means of oral speech into two types, from the point of view of their relation to the literary language, such as the lexicon of oral speech within the literary norm or close to the literary norm, and the means of oral speech that are not in the norm for the literary language and violate the norm when used in the literary language [76]. All types of verbal means, even rude, rude, swearing and cursing words are used in artistic speech and are aimed at performing a stylistic task. In this respect, the means of oral speech of a dialectal character stand out.

The writer's skill in using dialectics

An important part of oral speech is dialect and dialect words. Dialectisms are territorial words, and their source of use outside the dialect to which they belong is fiction. In works of art, dialectisms are mainly used for the purpose of individualizing the speech of the characters, reflecting the characteristics of a particular place. The artistic function of artistic dialectics is not limited to this.

Dialectisms are an integral part of the national language, and dialectisms found in works of art are the tools of a lively conversational speech of a representative of this nation. Since the heroes of the work of art represent such ordinary people, not

---

[76]Umurkulov B. Featured work. - B. 110 - 111.

using these tools in their speech leads to artificialization of the characters of the work, violation of the principles of time and space in the work. It seems that the use of dialectics in works of art is a necessity. Dialectisms are lexical tools specific to characters' speech and are an important resource that increases the vocabulary of literary language. It is a tool that organizes lexical diversity in works of art, with the help of which the language of the work of art is enriched and the folk character of the work is ensured. For this reason, writers pay special attention to the use of dialectics. The writer Murad Muhammad Dost is also a creative person who effectively used dialectics in his works. It can be observed that dialectisms are used in the writer's works, first of all, to show that the character of the work is a representative of the common people. This case shows the breadth of artistic function of dialectisms. For example, *in Mundaylik, I will be sob, uncle! - said Usmanali ("Mustafa")*, *the simple* dialectal words used in the speech show that the speaker is a representative of the common people. Because the dialectal words such *as "walking* like this" and " *sob* " meaning *"to be finished"* were used to show the character of the work, not the characteristic of a specific region. After all, these dialectal words are not specific to a certain region, but are used in several regions. - *You'll be right back from work, Saidboy. Or can't the government man speak louder? The dialectic of the soul* in the sentence ("Resignation") was used as a sign of the space reflected in the artistic work. This case shows that dialectisms in works of art are multi-functional. For example, dialectisms are used as synonyms of a certain word in the literary language, providing lexical diversity of artistic speech. Such words perform the task of giving a new form of meaning that is intended to be expressed. For example, *"Excuse me, Saidmurad Zamonovich," he said. - I spoke chakki, to put it bluntly, since you miss beauty* ("Resignation"), the dialectal word <u>chakki is a dialectal variant of the literary word nojoya</u> . The writer used this dialectic in the speech of a character representing the common people and chose a new form of expression. Therefore, the fundamental basis of the use of dialectics is that it is a means of expressing meaning.

Although the dialectisms found in the works of Murad Muhammad Dost have a number of characteristics, it can be observed that many dialectal words are used to express a certain meaning.

For example, *"Sit alone, you little mullah's son..." he shouted, Mahanboy. "A man should be careful!"* ("Return to Galatepa"), *On a good day, everyone is fine, on a bad day - hash* ("Resignation"), *If I'm kidding, I have a neck that suits me, what am I missing?!* ("Resignation"), *"Welcome," said Elomonov, and the dialectal words such as tek, mengzash, hash, bayinsa, iyib in* the sentences "Resignation" are primarily used as a means of expressing meaning in the text. It can also be observed that dialectisms found in the writer's works express several meanings and are used in methodologically specific cases. For example, *that's it* (...don't say that, teacher, - said *the* young man, *blushing . I... I do* n't *think so* .) as well as dialectal words such as *chatot, ovul, joyali, jon, gol, siyak, kek, tusmol* type, and words that are used in a dialectal manner by deliberately distorting phonetically and adapting it to oral speech, are also quite common . For example, the word *conductor* in the sentence "Lolazor" *asks, "Are you a conductor yourself, my son? "* In Yakshoboev's speech, the word conductor is deliberately distorted and given in the form of *a conductor , which brightened the hero's speech.* In terms of vocabulary, relying mainly on common words and means of oral speech ensured that the writer's works were linguistically simple, popular, expressive and attractive. For this purpose, it is possible to observe that in the works of the writer, dialectal variants of words typical of oral speech have been created. For example, *in the sentence "Ig'lamsirab spoke, his voice was healthy and his weight was not suitable for his weight"* ("Resignation"), the word " *unfit" compared to the variant "unfit" in the language* shows that it is suitable for this speech and, accordingly, it was used purposefully by the creator. Also, *he was not spared from exhaustion during the training. The word kularg* used in this text could also be used in the original language version of the text. However, a writer creates a new form without using an existing form in the language. The new *kularga word* created by the writer has the following characteristics. From the point of view of meaning expression, it is similar to the word *"laugh"*, both words do not have stylistic coloration from the point of view of meaning. It can be observed that the new construction has been given an oral, ordinary colloquial color only in terms of its usage. Based on this, the originality of this word in the text is assessed, first of all, by its coloring characteristic of ordinary speech, as well as by its different form of vocabulary.

Another dialectal word that expresses the individuality of the writer, reflecting the characteristics of ordinary colloquial speech, is the word *otlinkiramadi* . For example, *there was a hint of reproach in his voice, which did not sit well with Yakhaboev. - Try to be upset! - he threw the tube down with a thud.* ("Lolazor").

It is known that in Uzbek, the degree of lack of action understood from the verb is formed by adding suffixes such as -*nqira, -inqira, -msira, -imsira to the verb stem*. In general, the expression of the low level of action or sign is one of the main features of Murad Muhammad Dost's works. In the meaning of the word *otunkiramadi* given in the text , it is possible to observe the rarity of such a sign. It should be noted that the expression of a sign or an action in the diminutive state is also considered to be a situation characteristic of ordinary speech.

The writer managed to ensure the richness of the language of his work by effectively using these features of ordinary speech. The lack of movement is not expressed in the word *otunkiramadi* used in the above text . This word in the text has a completely new meaning *"did not like", "he did not like"* used in the meaning that it shows the skill of the writer in choosing words and using them in the text.

In his writings, the writer used the word " *cockerel* " to express the meaning of "crowling" . This word is also used to express several subtle meanings as an example of Murad Mohammad Dost's individual style. For example, *Mahanboy Soli glared at the butcher. The butcher was sitting idly.* In the sentence ("Return to Galatepa"), this word expresses the meaning of *"to beat" , "If you want to hit, let's hit!..."* Mullah *Soat shouted.* "Returning to Galatepa" *not to shout at the opponent,* to let him know that he is in a position to be equal to him, - *Shall I get permission from the elders? - said Orify* ("Lolazor") , the meaning of *showing off, boasting , He wiped his mouth with a towel, raised his head slowly, saw that Orify was standing a little cocky.* ("Lolazor") and in the sentence *"to show that he is capable of doing many things"* used to express its meaning, the writer's purpose in creating this word is to express the meaning of *"gerdaymak"* through various subtle meanings. According to the expression of such new meanings, the manifestation of the writer's individual skill of using words can be seen on the basis of the following dialectal words. One of the words used in the writer's works, which has acquired an important feature, *is mosquito* is the word - *If he talks again, you'll fly away! The patient stranger asked for this one book, if it was you.* ("Resignation"). The word *fly* in the writer's works , it is used in the meanings of *"to speak angrily"* and *"to mumble"* . The writer chooses this word due to the need to express the thought through one word, as there is no vocabulary unit in the form of a word that expresses these meanings. As a result of this need, one of the words created and used by the writer is the word *lied* . It is known that a very large part of creations created in artistic speech was created on the basis of interpretation of the meaning expressed by two words in one word. In such words, not only brevity is observed, but also attractiveness in relation to its meaning. If the artistic speech is based on the function of aesthetic impact, then formal compactness and attractiveness of words in terms of hearing and expressing meaning play an important role. In this respect, the use of *the word "lied"* is an example of the writer's skill in using dialectics: *"No, you know," he lied. Gaybarov - Let's not sit down to say something* ("Return to Galatepa"). *"I was just looking for a book for Sobirjon, "* he *lied* . In these texts, the compound word *"lied"* could also be used to express this meaning. This does not affect the overall meaning of the text. The writer's focus on choosing one of these two linguistic tools can be explained as follows. First of all, the meaning is expressed in a previously unexpressed form through the word *lied , and the speech is provided with a wealth of language tools.* Secondly, this word makes it possible to structure the speech in a compact way and is distinguished by the attractiveness of the form compared to its meaning. Writers who use words artistically use words, taking into account the meaning of the word, its connection with other words in the speech, as well as the shape and sound of the word, which correspond to the mentality of the receivers. This use of the word is a pledge to realize the main purpose of the writer. Professor N. Mahmudov A. While thinking about Qahhor's ability to use words, he noted that in the words used by the writer, in addition to the main meaning of the word, all its meanings and intricacies are clearly and distinctly visible, and that the meaning of the word completely adheres to the general event, situation, position of the writer, and the overall intonation of the *story* . based on its application. The scholar points out that the word [77] *"cloth" was used by the writer on the basis of choice due to the presence of the edge of meaning associated with discrimination .*

As a conclusion, it should be noted that although Murad Muhammad Dost's works contain a rich lexical content,

---

[77]Mahmudov N. On the linguopoetics of Abdulla Qahhor's stories // Uzbek language and literature - Tashkent, 1989, issue 4. - B. 34.

common words, colloquialisms and dialectisms stand out as important lexical tools in the writer's works.

THE LINGUOPOETIC NATURE OF PAREMAS
Semantic and linguopoetic features of idioms used in the writer's works

Idioms are figurative linguistic devices that appear as a product of human thinking. It can be observed that idioms are interpreted in the sources as a form of phraseological units. For example, the French linguist Sh. Balli considers idioms as phraseological units that form a whole based on the addition of words that have lost their original meaning semantically [78], while O.S. Akhmanova considers idiom (Greek: idiom-uniqueness) to be specific to a specific language and cannot be directly translated into other languages. interprets as language units [79]. In the explanatory dictionaries of linguistic terms of the Uzbek language, comments on the idiom are given in this context.

Idiom (Greek. specific expression, phrase). Representation of illogical thoughts, events, events. They are unique to a certain language and cannot be translated literally into other languages [80].

Although idioms and expressions are considered in the sources as linguistic units that arise based on the expression of

---

[78] Bally Sh. French stylistics. - M.: Inostra n nye literatury, 1961. - S. 344.
[79] Akhmanova O. S. Dictionary of linguistic terms. - M.: Soviet Encyclopedia, 1966. - P.165.
[80] Mahkamov N. Ermatov I. Explanatory dictionary of linguistic terms. - Tashkent: Science, 2013. - P.47.

figurative meaning, their different aspects are expressed in explanatory dictionaries of linguistic terms. Although the meaning seems to be changed in the expression of idioms, in fact, idioms are not words with a transferable meaning, but lexical units that arise based on the expression of a certain content in a new form by the owner of the language. Reflecting on the different characteristics of idioms and phraseological units, A. Yuldashev writes: "The difference between idioms and phraseological units is noticeable not only structurally, but also semantically-functionally and methodologically. The lexical meaning of IQS is not expressed through an image, but directly, and in phraseological units, reality is expressed through figurative meaning. The figurative meaning in the phraseological unit relies on the nominative meaning of the components [81]. Both idiom and phrase are units that express a meaning other than the original meaning of the word, which is formed based on the addition of words and the formation of words. Based on this situation, Sh.Rakhmatullaev shows that the phrase is a linguistic unit with content, but its meaning is not equal to the meaning expressed by the words in it [82]. This similarity in form and expression means that idioms and phrases are linguistic units close to each other in terms of form and

---

[81] Yuldashev A. A linguocognitive study of idiomatic conjunctions. - Tashkent, 2016. - B. 42 - 186.
[82] Rahmatullaev Sh. An explanatory phraseological dictionary of the Uzbek language. - Tashkent: Teacher, 1978. - B. 4.

content. Idioms are tools that show the ability of the speaker to use the language, which are used mainly in artistic speech, partly in oral speech, they are distinguished from other language tools mainly by their characteristic of individual use.

It is known that artistic speech is a speech based on figurative means. Based on the characteristics of artistic speech, the frequent use of idioms in this type of speech shows that these language units are figurative tools. Idioms are stable, indivisible lexical devices, such as idioms and proverbs, which are intended to express meaning as a whole. An idiom is a unique way of expressing meaning in a language, and the newly expressed meaning is not related to the lexical meaning expressed by the words forming the idiom. For example, - *You are right, comrade so-and-so. "I'm a person with a tongue "* ("Lolazor") is *a tongue-in-cheek* idiom *"I don't say anything"* used in the sense of This meaning is unrelated to the dictionary meaning of either word in the idiom. However, any lexical device expressing any meaning in the language must have a basis. It is on this basis that the speaker uses words to express a meaning. Idioms are linguistic devices resulting from this rationale. The word *"pishik"* in the quoted idiom is a unit of speech, when used alone, it means *"strong", "strong", "strong" in a figurative sense* . According to the expression *"strong"* this word is *a denotative twisted thread* and the connotative *mature person* expresses its meaning. In the next conjugation, the word *pishich is "thoughtful, one who knows his work, acts with judgment"* expresses the concept of a person. *It's ripe for the tongue* of the idiom It is this idiomatic meaning that emerges through the word *"pishik" that was an important basis* for its creation . Because a person who works with judgment and knowledge does not say anything. This case shows that the meaning of idioms, although it does not come from the meaning of the words in it, is related to the figurative meaning of one of the words in its component, the loss of the primary meaning of the words in idioms, the expression of a new meaning with this lexical tool is evidence that they are a unique means of expression in the language system. Idioms, like phrases, are figurative tools, and the fact that idioms play an important role in ensuring the artistic-imagery and richness of artistic speech can be clearly observed in the example of Murad Muhammad Dost's works. For example, the use of the *satanic laughter idiom* in the sentence "Lolazor" was an important means of expressing meaning for this text. Through this idiom , the meaning of *"Poisonous laughter"* is expressed, which means that the owner of the laughter is happy and has a bad attitude towards another person. *It is satanic laughter* to express this meaning in the text through any other lexical means could not convey the subtle meaning and emotionality of the idiom expression. Because in the sentence, it is thought about a person who made a big promise to complete the work, and therefore did not consider others, who set himself at a very high level. When it becomes clear that this work is absolutely impossible, the neglected person shows his joy. To express this situation, the writer uses the idiom of *satanic laughter* .

In this text, the hero's thoughts and happiness are continued based on his thoughts.

Through this combination, a strong level of the meaning of laughing at someone who humiliated himself, expressing his joy is expressed. Considering that it is not a characteristic of a person to be happy about someone else's defeat, the writer evaluates the situation by evaluating this situation as a characteristic of the devil. The idiom of *satanic laughter* has a linguopoetic meaning as a lexical tool that can express the inner experiences of the hero and the full attitude of the writer to these experiences.

You're out of luck, my golden girl, he thought, you left without paying attention to Yakshoboev, now you're inviting him, but Yakshoboev doesn't want to come in, you understand why, you're leaving. ("Lolazor"). The **idiom** in this sentence is also characteristic. This idiom actually means *"promising something one cannot do"* . What cannot be done cannot be done. Therefore, this idiom conveys the idea that you are doing something that cannot be done, although it is not stated openly. In terms of expression, both idioms used in the text are characteristic and lead to the expression of an impressive idea.

Through the idioms used in the work, the writer was able to reflect the purpose of his expression, the idea he put forward. For example, *he felt that Qurbanoy's hair was decreasing, he felt sorry for him, but he did not return from his previous determination.* In this sentence, two idioms *are reduced* and *the previous tense* is used. Although *Shashti knew that he was not capable of this task by shrinking , but he despised others, today* the idiom of his *previous determination is used to* express the meaning of *"no mercy"* . With this, the writer was able to vividly express his attitude towards hypocrisy to those who pretend to do what they cannot do.

Idioms create a unique expressiveness in the text with the emotional-expressiveness of the meaning understood from the idiomatic combination. In fact, idioms are also one of the rich possibilities of the national language, some of which were created by someone. The artist's skill in using words is determined by his ability to find such lexical tools that exist in the vernacular and use them in their place in speech. Idioms are also figurative tools, one of the idiomatic combinations rich in imagery is the idiom *you see your mother* . This idiom is figurative and impressive as it expresses the meanings of *"suffering"*, *"suffering"* on the basis of a high-level symbol. *"Don't lie, my dear Rahmatov,"* said Yakhaboev. - *In Bulduruk there is no spa. If you go in the same garmsel in cancer - you will see your real mother!* ("Lolazor"). The idiom *you will see your mother* in the text has the function of giving artistic color to the text , precisely because it expresses the meaning of *"to suffer"* .

You will see your mother **the high level of the concept of** *"to suffer" is expressed* in the idiom . *You will see* other lexical units expressing this meaning cannot convey the meaning expressed by the idiom. Idioms also play an important role in describing events in a clear and complete way before the eyes of the reader. Idioms are used to express actions and states based on modal relations, not to name things-phenomena in objective existence. Language tools that express modal relations always have the features of providing artistic and figurative. The speech, linguopoetic essence of idioms is determined by the fact that they provide expressiveness based on the creation of artistry and emotionality.

Idioms are formed as a result of the syntactic connection of several words, and in such a word connection, a certain word plays an important role in expressing the idiomatic meaning. For example, *Unexpectedly, I remembered the authority given by Osno, and my tongue was freed. I rained stones of rebuke on the heads of my comrades that education has weakened, young people are not paid attention to, and the result is that our young men who destroy the mountain sell trousers, and our girls sell pistachios ("Lolazor")* The idiom of *tushuv of my tongue in the text* is based on the expression of the word *tushuv* , which is typical of oral speech , meaning *"tied"* . In the text, this idiom is used in the sense of *"to speak"* . In the expression of the meaning of *"to speak", the word " dissolved "* in the compound is important, because without this word, first of all, the combination *of the language is abstract* in terms of meaning, it cannot express the meaning of *"to speak"* . Secondly, the meaning of this word is not just to speak, but *to "get into a conversation", to talk a lot* . In terms of expression, the idiom *of scolding stones in the text* is also characteristic. The meaning of the idiom is not related to the primary meanings of the words contained in the idiom, the text uses the idiom *of stones* to express *"critical thoughts"* . It seems that in the text, stones of reproach are used as a synonym for critical thought. Since the critical thoughts in the text are compared to a stone, this idiom is effective in relation to its meaning and has the ability to express the thought artistically and colorfully. The idiomatic expression "to not *speak* " is a means of speech. In the works of Murad Muhammad Dost, who effectively used the wide range of speech tools in his works, this idiom is used in the meanings of *"he spoke"* and *"he didn't speak"* . *In* the expression of the meaning of *"to speak"* , the words " *unfolded* " and in the expression of the meaning of *"did not speak"* performed an important task. For example, *I was afraid that our argument would turn into a dispute, fortunately, my grandson came and we started talking* ("Lolazor"). This case indicates the importance of grammatical status in the realization of the semantic meaning of idioms. A word that forms a specific meaning in connection with an idiom is absorbed into the composition of the idiom and expresses the specific meaning as a whole. In such cases, replacing the word contained in these components with another one leads to a change in meaning. This situation can be clearly seen in the example of the idioms " *I fell on my tongue" and "my tongue fell off"* . Idioms are basically specific lexical units in a language It is often used in artistic style as an expression of the meanings expressed on the basis of. It seems that idioms are a means of expressing a certain meaning in a new form, in this sense they are synonymous with a lexical unit in the language. The important aspect of cognates is that they represent different degrees of the meaning that is intended to be expressed by the word. The linguopoetic value of idioms is measured by the fact that they express meaning at different levels, and that they are a new means of expressing these meanings. The meaning of the language in the given example has been solved, it is not just that you *want to speak, it is different from its counterparts in the language that expresses the same* meaning, and it acquires a linguopoetic essence according to the nature of expression. *"Speak"* in the writer's works and to express the meaning of *"not to speak"* , the idiomatic expressions <u>*"to bite the tongue "* and *"to hold the tongue"*</u> are also used, and it is seen that these idioms also express a subtle meaning. For example, *Then my tongue itched badly. I wanted to say that, Oh, Oshno, I will be the one who hastened Moira! I restrained my tongue, later I realized that I did the right thing* ("Lolazor") In the text, the idiom " *my tongue itches* " is "I wanted to say", hold your tongue "I didn't say, I didn't speak" used in meanings such as It seems that *the idioms used in the writer's writings, idioms to itch the tongue, hold back the tongue, I didn't have my tongue (...The neighbors heard me, their lips hung open, but I didn't have the tongue to apologize.* "Lolazor" *)* were used to express the same meaning at different levels. This situation is an example of the writer's skill in using language units for different purposes.

An important aspect of idioms is that they do not exist in a standard state in the language system, they are characteristic of speech. Accordingly, the formation of idioms is related to the activity of a person, and the large number of idioms in the works of a certain writer indicates the high skill of the creator in creating words. Because idioms are lexical units that are structurally innovative in terms of their structure, which are created illegally for language norms. They do not conform to the norms of the literary language in terms of their structure, they do not have an explicit (open) expression. Accordingly, idioms can be called language units with implicit (hidden) expression.

Idioms are formed in the form of a word combination, their formation syntactically corresponds to the norms of the literary language, and when analyzed from a lexical point of view, the combination of two words does not express any specific lexical meaning. Because the words in idioms do not have meaning related to the lexical meaning that these words represent. The meaning expressed by idioms is inextricably linked with the text in which this tool is used, and the meaning of the idiom is realized in connection with the content of the text.

The source of idioms in the Uzbek language is oral and artistic speech, and the existence of a number of idioms found in artistic texts can be felt in oral speech, in ordinary conversation. The unique properties of such units create the basis for their inclusion in artistic texts. For example, *Izbosarov is a great guy, he said. - He does not leave his position, he does not leave his position* in the sentence ("Resignation"). If the meaning of the compound is formed on the basis of the dictionary meaning of the words in the compound, it does not have a clear concept. Since the meaning of the words in this idiom is completely disconnected from the meaning of the words, *he will do what he says, he will do what he says* , and this meaning has an implicit expression in this idiom in connection with the text. Or, if the idiom "My mouth is burnt" in the sentence " *My mouth is burned , it's hard to believe in a sweeter word* " ("Resignation") *expresses the meaning of suffering in this text* , then in another text, the combination of " *mouth is burned* " may be used in the correct sense, and it may not be an idiom, because the combination of *"mouth is burned"* means a hot meal. when burning the mouth by consumption is expressed, this expression corresponds to the general meaning of the components of the compound. *"Scald of the mouth" by means of a scalded* compound . and the expression of the meanings of *"suffering" is evidence of its presence in the speech in the form of a word combination and an idiomatic combination.* The emergence of an idiom is connected with the need for figurative and artistic expressive expression of thought. Because an idiom names a thing-phenomenon, an action-state that is not originally a term, comparing it based on understanding the similar aspects of another thing-event, action-state. Such language units have strong descriptive and descriptive properties compared to other words. As a result, the thought expressed through these means can acquire an artistic effect . For example, *Elomonov restrained his imagination and got busy for breakfast* ("Resignation"), *the* word *restrained* in the idiom combination of his imagination is not characteristic of imagination. The emergence of this idiom is related to the figurative expression of thought, created on the basis of concepts in the imagination. For the creation of an idiom, the limitlessness and breadth of human imagination is compared to the movement of a galloping horse. A galloping horse must be restrained. In essence, idioms are actually ambiguous, their meaning is determined only when they are compared to other things, for example, the combination of *"bridle your imagination"* does not express a clear meaning, its meaning is realized in a state of comparison. This shows the uniqueness of idioms as important language units that are not visible on the surface. Consequently, the meaning expressed by an idiom is wider than the expression in the ordinary case. Because the meaning of idioms is not the original dictionary meaning, it is a hidden meaning, that is, a new meaning expressed in order to organize the artistic effect of the work based on the figurative thinking of the creator. The formation of a certain meaning through idioms is a relative phenomenon, and it depends on the creator's ability to perceive the world, linguistic skill in defining and describing the world. Idioms, as unique linguistic units in terms of formation and expression, can acquire important features in the speech process. The creation of idioms and their widespread use in artistic speech is due to the fact that they can express a subtle meaning and are a new means of expression.

    The writer Murad Muhammad Dost is a creator who used idioms as well as other vocabulary units. Idioms found in the writer's work can be divided into traditional and individual idioms. Traditional idioms are well-known units that exist in speech, and are determined by the presence of imagery in the semantics of their use in speech. For example, idioms such as *frowning, frowning, qiil sigmay (to the heart) are actively used in oral speech* to express a person's upset state . In the works of the writer, there are cases where these expressions are used to express different situations and convey a subtle meaning. Usually *to frown, to frown* the pallor on the face of a person who is upset about something is a unit that is comparable to the hanging of a pumpkin. Accordingly, these lexical devices represent the state of grief. This situation can be expressed through the words *sad, very sad in the language, but it does not describe a person, the signs of his sadness are not visible in front of a person's eyes.* In this respect, the speech characteristics of these idioms are revealed. It seems that the creation of these idioms is directly related to the comparison of things, the description and the artistic coloring of the thought as a result of the description. Also, in the semantics of idioms, the meaning is sometimes hidden. In the works of Murad Muhammad Dost, these idioms are not used in the sense of sadness, but in the sense of putting oneself in this situation. For example, *I have read, - said Yakhasboev, frowning even more, and then reprimanded the mahmadona. In the sentence "You can write it without reading it* " ("Lolazor"), the expression of displeasure with the interlocutor's speech is expressed through the idiom of *frowning* . In this place, the state of resentment is not felt, but there is a state of dissatisfaction with the opinion of the interlocutor. Or - *No, I'm just like that, - said Gaybarov, frowning,* and in the sentence ("Return to Galatepa"), this idiom was used to show his natural intensity, the severity of his character. Yakh *Shiboyev also frowned, bowed his head, as if he was suffering from* infinite *sadness* . To express this mental state in a person, the idiom *"can't do enough"* is also used. This lexical unit is also commonly used in oral speech and artistic texts. In terms of expression, it is equal to the lexical means listed above, that is, it expresses cases of extreme sadness. For example, *Elomonov laughed when he heard this statement, even though he was not happy with it* ("Resignation"). The expressions *"frowning" , "frowning" and "satisfying",* which are similar in expression of "disgust", confirm the existence of semantic features in idioms. In the writer's works, many idioms, which are characteristic of traditional usage, such as *to put a foot on the face, to avoid talking, to lose one's head, to be my aunt's calf, to stiffen the neck, to fall out of the eyes, to be a board, to be noticed, to have a bad mouth, to have a long tongue, to have short hands, to have sharp eyes,* express certain meanings in a non-traditional way . according to which provided artistic impression. The fact that these idioms do not correspond to the usual combinations in terms of syntactic and structure, and do not express the original meaning of one of the words in the combination is the basis for the expression of an artistic idea. For example, the words in the idiom *to split the board* do not mean anything based on their original meaning in the text.

In the meaning of the idiom, it is important to compare the situation with something else, the situation. *Binafshakhan waited for disaster if he expected it, but because he didn't think about it, he became a board* ("Resignation"), the character's situation is described on the basis of comparing it to a board. *He was stuck* in expressing this meaning idiom is also used, and the comparison of the unchanging, stable state of a person at a certain time with an object and another state led to the formation of idioms.

Although idioms are combinations of two or more existing words in a language, they are new words that are completely different from their constituent words. For example, *short-handed* when the combination is used in relation to the original meaning of the words in this combination, it means the shortness of the hand in terms of measurement, and it has the opposite meaning in relation to the combination *of the long hand . He is short-handed* **the use** of the idiom in the meaning of *"poor", "not able to do many things"* means that it is another lexical unit, *a short hand that indicates a measure* shows that it has a formative relationship with the compound. The creation of a specific lexical unit in the language takes place based on the general grammatical features of the language. In this, special attention is paid to the process of expressing the meaning in the mind and imagination of the lexical tool. There is no doubt that the creation of many lexical tools involves the figurative perception of the world, the telling of messages about things and events in an effective way to people. Idioms are such language units and are evidence of the creation of idioms based on the wealth of folk wisdom and the world of thought of the people. The writer Murad Muhammad Dost skillfully used such examples of folk wisdom in his works and was a creator who was able to create new idioms. In the writer's works, one can find many idioms that are a product of the folk tradition, used on the basis of individual skills, and have acquired a linguopoetic essence with the characteristic of expressing a subtle meaning. For example, *Ogil Raim was the son of the elder, he lied, but told the truth: now, the soil of the father and the daughter will be emptier* ("Return to Galatepa"). The component of *the empty soil idiom* used in reference to a person contains a word that serves to express a characteristic characteristic of a person in terms of meaning. For example, the existence of a scheme to interpret human character in the sense of the word *"empty"* may have been the basis for the formation of this idiom. Such idioms, which do not correspond to the pattern of word combinations of the literary language according to the original meaning of the words in the combination, which seem silly to attribute to a person from the point of view of form, are undoubtedly tools that provide emotionality in terms of expression. An important word that shapes the meaning of an idiom is the word *empty* . Through this word, there is a hint that the signs of the female character are gentleness, kindness, trustworthiness of a woman, not always feeling the need for independent thinking when making decisions. A lexical unit representing this concept does not exist in the language. Accordingly, the idiom *of empty soil* attracts attention as an important lexical unit expressing this concept. The function of many idioms in the speech system is determined by the feature of expression, since idioms are often a means of expressing concepts that do not have a language representative. It is known that the use in the meaning of naming language units is common, and as a result of the selection of forms that express different meanings in artistic texts, the language becomes lexically enriched, the main part of such tools is distinguished by its speech specificity and creates various methodological possibilities. Therefore, lexical units of this type are considered as speech units, and their main function is determined by the fact that they are characteristic of speech. Idioms are also such speech units that create various speech possibilities and motivate their creation. For example, *to collect laughter (But he caught sight of Koklamov, who was in the corner of the room, near the sideboard, who had finished his work and was wondering what to do, and laughed.* "Lolazor" *)* an unusual expression from the point of view of language. Because the word *to collect* does not have the same valence as the word *laugh* , *to collect* when used with definite object nouns, it expresses the meaning according to the norms of the language: *to clean the house, to collect one's belongings* . Accordingly, the word *"gathering"* in the compound " *gathering* " means " *laughter"* connected with the word and *pretending to be upset* expressed the meaning. This indicates that this lexical device expresses a new meaning. This is evidence that idioms are tools for creating new meaning in the speech process. Expressing new meanings by creating idioms is related to the creator's perception, understanding of the world, and finding an appropriate vocabulary tool for expressing the perceived things. The meaning *of the expression to gather laughter* is characteristic of the writer's individual style, and it is based on the expression of the expression of the mouth wide open when laughing, the faces light up with joy, and when sad, the opposite of this situation occurs, that is, the lips hang down, and the mouth is in its natural state . and was able to logically express the meaning of this text. It seems that idioms do not simply express meaning, but come into the field as a means of describing human things, events, their actions unknown to others, drawing conclusions from observations and describing them.

    Idioms are also created in the process of expressing concepts that are based on human thinking. A person gives a new name to other concepts based on the fact that he compares various things in life with things in his mind. So are many idioms it can be observed that it was created on the basis. For example, *no* the word is used in relation to a person and is used in relation to people who do not keep their word and do not keep their promises. People who have not found their place in life, and their work has not progressed, often complain about life. He blames the world for not laughing at him. When comparing these situations, the writer uses the *famous idiom of the world . In your imagination, you will be a bird, not so much a bird, Sorburgut! You will fly, you will fly, you will fly, you will fly from the beginning to the end of the poor world!* The *idiom of the infamous world* in the sentence ("Return to Galatepa") represents the world that did not bring good to the imaginary person and did not allow him to find his place in life. This expression was formed as the basis of the comparison of the world with the person who does not do good to a person, and acquired a linguopoetic essence due to the fact that it can be the name of a new concept in the mind. In this respect, *Tagi is rotten! - Mrs. Muhsina said happily, - he was my enemy, he left, it's surprising.* The idiom *rotted* in the sentence ("Lolazor") is also characteristic. The word *ketibdi* in this sentence expresses the mobile meaning of *"fired"* . *The bottom is rotten* commonly used for a tree whose trunk has rotted from near the root. In this text, the combination of *"root rotted" and "root rotted"* in relation to a tree cannot be considered a single linguistic unit. These tools, which are the same in form, express different meanings. The appearance of the next one was a direct result of thinking based on a person's understanding of the world, comparison of things and events with others, and was used in the sense of *"a lot of hard work"* . A tree with a rotten base gradually rots away, and a person whose affairs are revealed, when they are revealed, is released from his duty. This is the basis of the idiom, and based on the comparison of the results , the idiom *rotten at the bottom is used, and the text is given an artistic spirit.*

If the creation of idioms is based on the perception of the creator, the sense of the connection of the meaning to be expressed with another thing-event, the artistry of such expressions becomes stronger. Expressing a meaning, a concept in a text that has not been expressed before, always becomes a means of providing artistry and impressiveness. The creation of new words in literary texts, the expression of figurative meanings, the use of words expressing several meanings is determined by creating certain possibilities in the text. Idioms are such linguistic units, which correspond to the requirements of the artistic text with their linguistic novelty. For example, because the formation of the idiom of <u>*the sentence runaway*</u> is unconventional, it seems new to a person, because the sign of running away is not a characteristic of the sentence, but the word *runaway* is important in the formation of the meaning of this idiom. Based on this idiom expressing the meaning of disagreement, there is a concept that people who disagree do not communicate with each other, do not talk. It is this concept that prepared the ground for the formation of the idiom . (...*Uncle Naim sensed that the conversation had slipped out of the middle.* "Return to Galatepa") or *the conversation (Rakhmatli's mother was not one of those women who had a conversation inside her, she immediately conveyed the conversation to her daughter* . It is caused by the fact that he says even if it is forbidden, and in some cases, the opposite of this situation exists. *To lie* in the formation of the meaning of the idiom that *does not lie in it* **It was an important basis that** the word was directed to express the meaning of *"to keep"* . This idiomatic combination has the same meaning as the combination of *"to keep secret" in the language* , and it is significant in terms of its emotional-expressiveness, expressed in a new form. The analysis of existing materials shows that in the formation of idioms, even if the original meaning of the words in the idiom component is not expressed, a new meaning is created through the original meaning of any word in its composition, as a result of comparing it to other things based on this meaning. For example, *since Binafshakhan made a bad prediction, the moment came when Elomonov also had a problem. The clause* in the sentence ("Resignation") *is to turn* **The meaning expressed by the word** *turn* in the idiom was the basis for the emergence of the meaning expressed by the idiom.

This situation led in the expression of meaning of idioms found in the works of the writer Murad Muhammad Dost. The writer's idioms expressing idiomatic meaning in relation to the sentence word *do not lie, do not lie, do not lie, do not lie, do not lie , do not lie, do not lie* Even if the lexical meaning of the words is not expressed in the idiom, these words are the ones that form the meaning of the idiom. Because the meaning of these words refers to another situation. For *example , "You tell a lot of lies," Binafshakhan said, hanging on her husband's words (* " Resignation") . The first is "quick" in colloquial speech . means, accordingly, *"to take quickly,"* secondly, *to pick up a thrown object without dropping it* is used in the sense of In general, the main meaning of this compound is *"to get"* , and the meaning is expressed through this word. In the idiom expression *to hang up the words, the* word that is important for expressing the meaning is the word to hang up . The idiom expresses the meaning of *"he didn't stop talking", "he didn't speak", and he took away what he wanted to say and spoke by himself* . One of the important aspects of an idiom is the complexity of understanding the meaning of an idiom. It is determined by the fact that the meaning of idiomatic compounds does not depend on the meaning of the words in it and shows the essence of the idiom. For example, it is illogical to understand the combination *of stepping on the face* in the sense expressed by the words in it. Because this is not the case in life. However, some behaviors are compared to this state, resulting in an enhanced meaning. For example, the idiomatic combination *"I despised, despised"* in the sentence *"Akalari didn't talk back to me, but they stepped on my face"* ("Return to Galatepa") expresses the meaning of "I despised, despised." determined by provision. Or Elomonov *restrained his imagination and was busy eating breakfast* ("Resignation") The meaning of the idiom could be expressed through the combination of *thinking* . However, *if* it is a simple form of expression, *it* can give an artistic spirit to the thought. Idioms as a lexical unit are characterized by the fact that speech is a means of providing artistic-imagery of thought. For example, *Elomonov himself, a local star who is still in his career, patted the head of the young man a couple of times, and told the guests that he has a future* in ("Resignation"). **The use of the idiomatic combination** *of the brighter star* in expressing the meaning was an important tool for the effective reception of the idea.

In general, idioms are complex language units in terms of the unconventional structure and the connection of the meaning of the lexical tools with the new meaning expressed by the idiom. The essence is the basis for the formation of idioms as separate units of their own, and created the basis for their creation and use in certain types of speech. One of the main sources of idioms is artistic speech, and it can be seen that many individual idioms are used in artistic works, which strengthen the artistic character of the work and provide figurative artistry. One of such creators is the writer Murad Muhammad Dost, whose works use idioms as well as all linguistic tools, which shows that these lexical units have an important role in the speech process.

Linguistic features of folk proverbs in the writer's works

Proverbs are an example of folk wisdom, and proverbs express people's observations and accumulated rich experience. There are poets and writers, eloquent and eloquent, old and young, who certainly turn to proverbs when they want to substantiate or strengthen their opinion. An idea expressed in a proverb cannot be replaced by any means of language or justified at the level of a proverb [83]. The creation of proverbs is related to the evaluation of things based on a deep understanding of life, drawing conclusions as a result of mutual comparison of events. Accordingly, proverbs are an example of a high way of thinking, in which instructive thoughts are expressed in a concise, understandable way. An important feature of proverbs is the expression of people's life, people's lifestyle, customs, dreams, and spiritual world in the spirit of giving morals based on experiences. The moral, spiritual and

---

[83]Joraeva B. Linguistic foundations of the formation of Uzbek folk proverbs. - Tashkent: Akademnashr, 2019. - B. 3.

educational views of this nation are expressed in every folk proverb. In this respect, proverbs appear as an expression of the spirit of the people. The subject range of folk proverbs is wide and varied, because proverbs are created by the people, and all aspects of life are expressed in them.

Proverbs are a means of expressing thought in concise, figurative, artistic colors, and are a form of expression designed to convey the thought to the listener in an effective way. The proverb is explained as follows in the "Annotated Dictionary of the Uzbek Language". *A concise, figurative, meaningful and wise expression, sentence, created by the people based on life experience, usually has a teaching content* [84]. Proverb researchers have recognized that proverbs are pandnoma-like opinions consisting of artistic and figurative opinions arising from people's life experience. For example, in "Hikmatnama" - "Explanatory dictionary of Uzbek proverbs" proverbs are described in this way. "Proverbs can be called an "encyclopedia of life", a verbal encyclopedia, a kind of artistic historical chronicle. They sharpen people's minds, make their speech fluent and impressive, teach them how to choose the right path in life, solve life's puzzles and problems correctly, give advice

---

[84] An explanatory dictionary of the Uzbek language. - Tashkent: National Encyclopedia of Uzbekistan, 2006. - B. 569.

on all major and minor issues of life [85]. Proverbs are stable in the structure of the language, and the expression of figurative meaning is one of the important features of proverbs. Proverbs are ready-made syntactic devices that express a grammatically completed thought, in this sense they are equivalent to a sentence. Proverbs exist in a stable combination and are language units that are used ready-made in speech and are used mostly unchanged when used in literary texts. This case indicates that the proverbs are known to everyone and are used in a traditional way. The use of proverbs in literary texts is related to their speech functions. In Uzbek classical works, the art of using proverbs with a goal in mind is said to *be a hereditary parable* . One of the founders of classical poetry, Atullah Hosseini, said about the proverb: "According to the popular saying, one verse should be included in one verse. This can be done in two ways. The first and best way is to give the parable without changing the words and order, and the second way is to change the parable [86]. "

Proverbs are multifunctional in speech, they are used both for communicative purpose and as an artistic and aesthetic tool. Because proverbs are created as a product of the artistic thinking of the people, they summarize the knowledge of nature

---

[85] Shomaksudov Sh., Shorahmedov Sh. Wisdom. Explanatory dictionary of Uzbek proverbs. - Tashkent: 1990 B. 8.
[86] Atullah Hosseini. Badoyi'u-s-sanoyi'. - Tashkent: Literature and art named after G'. Ghulam, 1981. - B. 135.

and society and express it in a concise form. That is the reason why proverbs are alive and equally suitable for all eras.

The use of proverbs in works of art is also traditional, Gulkhani's work "Zarbulmasal" is famous as a work decorated with proverbs [87]. Proverbs do not remain a means of expressing thoughts in works of art, but provide the effectiveness of the work, the artistic-imagery of the thought, increase the artistic-aesthetic level, and arouse pleasure in the reader. The linguopoetic essence of proverbs is determined by these aspects.

Proverbs are a means for the creator to realize his idea, to justify his thoughts, and to create an artistic effect. The use of proverbs in artistic speech arises from the demand of the speech situation, and the creator uses the proverb, which is a source of advice created by the people, to prove and demonstrate the idea he wants to express, and gives artistic color to the idea. Although the basis of the proverb is based on denotativeness, the use of some of the words in its content in figurative sense, the understanding of the proverb in a figurative sense, expression of thoughts based on comparison with things-subjects, references to other things-events, creation of a state of demonstrability, creates the ground for the shift of such lexical tools to the connotative meaning. That is why there are artists who pay special attention to the use of folk proverbs in their

---

[87] http:// www.ziyouz.com_library. Gulkhani "Zarbolmasal". -Tashkent, "Teacher Publishing House". 1972.

works of art. Scientist P. Bakirov, who is specially engaged in the semantic and structural features of proverbs, shows 10 main signs that distinguish proverbs from other paremiological units [88]. Among these signs, the following features that indicate that proverbs are used for artistic speech should be noted. Proverbs are popular, ancient in terms of origin, important according to their use, metaphorical, ambiguous and generalizable, structural-semantic completeness, figurative, and poetic aspects ensure that proverbs meet the requirements of artistic speech, and there is a need to use proverbs for artistic speech that embodies these features. Proverbs are paremiological units that perform the function of demonstrativeness in artistic speech. After all, proverbs used in artistic texts are directed to focus on the meaning understood from the proverb. The use of folk proverbs can be observed in the works of all artists, but the work of the writer Murad Muhammad Dost stands out in using proverbs in his works and creating different versions of proverbs. In the works of the writer, it can be observed that proverbs are used with several functions. For example, - *I have never heard of a time when the master-student was burdened. It is clear that* the syntactical device " The old man knows , *the man does not know"* in the sentence "The old man knows, the man does not know" means that the old man knows many things. Based on the

---

[88]Bakirov P.U. Semantics and structure nominatsentricheskih poslovits. - Tashkent: Science, 2006. - B. 15. 22.

expression of this meaning, it is indicated that an old person has lived for many years, has witnessed many things in life, and thinks based on experiences. In this syntactic device, the comparison of the old man with the theonymic fairy is aimed at creating imagery. The use of this proverb in the text served to provide evidence for the point to be made. In other words, the fact that the old man's knowledge is strengthened by the image of a fairy as proof of the idea that it is necessary to accept the teachings of the teacher and do what he says shows the presence of figurative perception in this expression. That is why creators use such linguistic tools as a means of ensuring artistic-impressiveness. The use of lexical tools in speech, which have artistic and aesthetic possibilities in the form and content of the language, is related to their selection and matching with the content and essence of the speech. On the contrary, if the tools with artistic color are not used in their place in the speech, they spoil the speech and lead to the emergence of logically unrelated thoughts. This situation is observed, first of all, in paremas, including the use of proverbs and sayings. Proverbs, matal are lexical units that have artistic, expressiveness in a certain sense. In proverbs, this feature arises based on the expression of figurative meaning, and in matals, it is manifested by the fact that it has the character of admonition, some words in their content have figurative meanings, comments are made on the basis of comparison of things and events, and they are used with a number of other characteristics in mind. Accordingly, the use of parema types in artistic texts is based on their stylistic possibilities. For example, *if I didn't get together in time, then we have more children without melting - the burden is now falling on my shoulders. No, that was nonsense. If there are ten - another place, if there are a hundred - guidance* ("Lolazor") This proverb created in the spirit of our nation's respect for children and expressing love for them is understood in the correct sense. However, at the heart of its creation, together with the expression that our nation is a young nation, the presence of the meaning of paying attention to the fact that each person has his place in life determines the main essence of the proverb. That is, each child is unique in terms of its character, behavior, external signs, as well as in intelligence and behavior. This life truth is expressed in the content of the proverb. The use of the proverb in this text is related to the idea that *we have multiplied children - the burden is now falling on our shoulders* . To prove the wrongness of this idea, this proverb that each person has his own life path was used. And in places where the child is not considered, the use of this proverb does not correspond to the essence. It seems that when using a linguistic tool in the text, it is also intended to highlight the idea to be expressed. The quoted text has a complete meaning without this proverb. However, the meaning understood from the proverb was absorbed into the content of the text based on the use of this tool and gave it an additional meaning. This is evidence that proverbs can perform several tasks in the text at the same time. If the quoted proverb performed a denotative function according to its correct meaning, the presence of relational, argumentative meanings in the structure of the proverb served to ensure the emotional color of the thought.

Like other linguistic tools, proverbs name an object, thing-phenomenon in the process of communication and interaction with the interlocutor. Being able to be a figurative expression of the thing-phenomenon on the basis of figurative meaning ensures that it fulfills an artistic and aesthetic task. For example, the proverb used in the sentence " *Yes, now it's worth his ass , brother, if I'm a person who leaves"* nominative has an artistic-aesthetic value in terms of expressing the meaning of evaluation based on the transfer of meaning, and expressing this meaning based on comparison. When using a proverb in artistic texts, the compatibility of the proverb with the content of the text is considered an important basis for the expression of an artistic idea. In the cited text, the comparison of the person separated from his duty to the subject in the proverb in terms of status and status was based on the compatibility of the proverb and the text. The meaning of treating the leader, leaders, and common man according to the content of the sentence is explained based on the use of the proverb "Treat like a donkey . " It seems that the proverb provided the brightness of the thought to be expressed in harmony with the content of the text. The transfer of meaning in it, the explicit expression of the thought in the proverb, the comparison of objects that are not of the same type strengthened the artistic impression. When linguistic tools are used for artistic purposes in artistic texts, special importance is attached to their compatibility with the direction of speech. This is even more evident in the use of proverbs. Because within the framework of communicative and artistic-aesthetic functions of proverbs, speech opportunities such as compatibility of the content and meaning of the text, vivid embodiment of the idea that the writer wants to express, are embodied. This situation, in turn, creates complications in the use of proverbs in artistic texts. For this reason, using proverbs to create thoughts and images and express artistic ideas is rare even in works of art.

It can be observed that proverbs are used for the following purposes in the works of Murad Muhammad Dost.

a) in the sense of showing the advantage of this activity in order to work together. *Let's build a great future together. They say that a divided person is a wolf, let us not be divided or wolves, let us be united* ("Lolazor"). In this sentence, a proverb is used to show the superiority of activities leading to unity over individual activities. The characteristic thing is that the proverb is not only a means of expression, but also created visuality in this place. Demonstrating the extent of the situation of a divided person through the image of a wolf, promoting unity and solidarity created the basis for the use of this proverb for the realization of an artistic idea.

b) proverbs are also used in texts intended to give advice, solve problems, and express opinions in the context of showing the right path.

For example, *You do it right, brother Elomonov. One death in one head, one should not be afraid The proverb one death in one head in* the sentence ("Resignation") encourages the character to act without fear, to do his job. The main idea that comes from the content of the proverb is that if there is one death, then everyone has it. Therefore, a person should fight for the well-being of his life without thinking about it. Or *he gathered the leaders of the Oasis and said that he was worried about the harvest, that our growers should be diligent, that it is a man's job to keep his promise* ("Lolazor"). This proverb is used to refer to a promise to fulfill a task. The content of the proverb has the character of admonition and urges a person to be correct and to speak up about what he said.

c) proverbs are also used in order to guide a person to the right path and to draw conclusions by stating the facts of life. For example, *"When a camel needs a saddle, it stretches its neck, my child." By quoting the saying "Tell the director that* 's it" ("Lolazor"), it was emphasized that everyone should try to live by himself. The proverb is based on real life. In fact, the denotative meaning of a camel stretching its neck to suck is understood from the proverb. An important feature of the proverb is that this situation is compared to the activity of a person, and the connotative meaning of the fact that a person needs to act in order to live is compared to the movement of a camel. It seems that in proverbs, two-sided meaning is expressed, unexpressed content is embodied. As a result of the artist's skill in artistic texts, the colorful features of proverbs are manifested in an artistic form.

g) when proverbs are used in the characters' speech, they have the function of expressing the character's reaction to the event. *Journalism is beyond me. Even if the sparrow is slaughtered, let the butcher slaughter it himself* ("Resignation"), the speaker's inability to do journalism means that he is not an expert in this field. The quoted proverb refers to the fact that everyone should do what he can. *"I cry not for my belly, but for my value, my child," says Mrs. Muhsina, turning to Ollayor*.

When expressing a reaction to a certain thing-event, when evaluating a person, folk proverbs are used to confirm an opinion, to show the characteristic of a thing-event or a person. For example, *it is true that it gives on the one hand and hits on the other. Haykal Ganievich did not hesitate to say that the proverb mentioned in the sentence ("Lolazor") is used in the speech of a character who is struggling with his work and sometimes has problems, and* expresses his attitude to life. In the sentence, this proverb is used in order to prove that all of them are bad, it is used to express the opinion based on comparison, and the proverb has a connotative function, as it means the concept of *"All evildoers are bad" in the figurative sense.*

d) proverbs in the writer's works are mainly aimed at the listener's imagination of the thought understood from the text with all its subtlety. The points to be expressed are proved on the basis of proverbs. For example, *grass to grass, water to water (- Grass to grass, water to water... muttered Yakhaboev. "Lolazor")* the opinion that the wealth found in an honest way brings happiness to a person, and on the contrary, the wealth found in an impure way leads to bad consequences, is proved by citing this proverb. The proverb creates an idea about the consequences of accumulating wealth by honest and impure means.

Proverbs found in the writer's works can be divided into groups such as folk variant, modified and occasional proverbs specific to the writer's individual style. Proverbs used in the form of a folk variant are rare in writer's works, when using a number of proverbs, some sounds are added or words are added, sometimes morphemes are changed, sometimes proverb variants are created. The method of conveying the thought expressed in the writer's works to the reader is the basis for using proverbs as they are or with modifications. Proverbs are used literally if the writer intends to prove the point he wants to express. For example, *Grass is to grass, water is to water, Faithful to a promise is the work of a man, On one side he gives, on the other side he hits, Shame is stronger than death* ("Lolazor"), *There are those who have reached their mouths and those who have not* ("Resignation"), *White dog, black dog, proverbs such as bari bir it* ("Return to Galatepa") are used to confirm the expressed idea, in the use of proverbs of this type, although they are artistically created based on the presence of figurative meaning, there is emotional-expressive coloring, a more communicative task prevails. After all, the basis of the use of all language tools in speech is related to the communicative process, and proverbs are no exception. However, the presence of a sign in the meaning of a proverb indicates that the stylistic capabilities of proverbs have a dual function, unlike words used for communicative purposes.

In the case of adverbs used without modification, the following cases are observed in the case of adverbs used without modification.

In the writer's works, when proverbs are used as the characters' own words, morphemes are changed, sometimes words are added. For example, *it will snow for the rest of the work, elder, he said. -If you tell me the topic of the upcoming conversation, I will prepare accordingly...* ("Lolazor"). *He colluded with his friends and killed his mother every day. Now is a different time.* Proverbs such as "Ready Uzadi, Unread Tozadi" ("Return to Galatepa") are used as characters' words in the text. *What's wrong with me if you fail? Do you burn the blanket by pissing off the fleas?* When using the proverb ("resignation"), the morphemic change in the proverb is the result of the character using the proverb as his own word. Proverbs used in modified form are also used in order to emphasize the situation and strengthen the meaning understood from the proverb. For example, *the chorus brought by Water - he, the saint who broke the jar! Why was I released? So many years of my services are void?* The proverb quoted in the sentence ("Lolazor") is used with the addition of the preposition *u* . This proverb has two propositions in terms of syntactic structure and is built on the basis of contradictory meaning. The inconsistency of the characters in the proposition is the essence of the proverb and has an artistic-aesthetic value by figuratively expressing the concept of "the rightly walking choir, the wrongly walking saint" in the image of the one who brought water and broke the jug. Because in it, the good things in life are not always evaluated as good, the bad ones are not evaluated as bad, the vital fact that there are often inconsistencies in the assessment is expressed, attention is drawn to this situation, and conclusions are indicated.

It seems that in addition to the general meaning of the proverb, the meaning of emphasis is embodied in proverbs. It was used by the writer as an addition - *it* served to strengthen the meaning of emphasis and draw special attention to it. In this way, the creator increased the artistic and aesthetic essence of the proverb. In general, in proverbs, drawing attention to the content of the proverb and strengthening its meaning by adding the preposition " *u" is one of the features of Murad Muhammad Dost's works.* This situation can also be observed in the use of the following proverbs.

- *Oh, our heads are bald, our hearts are tender!* - said *Binafshakhan* ("Resignation"). *Okay, brother, we have power, we don't have power* ("Lolazor"). The meaning understood from the proverb is emphasized and strengthened by using some additions in the proverb. At the same time, in some cases, it is intended to express a subtle meaning. For example, ... *there was a little lightness in his voice, a tone of hope, forty-day greetings in the place where you once ate salt...* ("Lolazor"). The use of this proverb is also consistent with the writer's individual style of expression. The proverb has an expression in the form of the inner speech of the hero of the work, and the suffix *-like is added* to the word *kun* , and the change of the proverb is based on the idea that the proverb wants to express in the imagination, that is, the hero is waiting for salvation from the person who was in this house before, for the sake of bread and salt. manifested.

In the works of the writer, there are also those whose form has been changed while preserving the main content expressed in the folk proverb.

For example, *"Don't be a sultan in a foreign country, be a sultan in your own country!..."* ("Lolazor") has a mainly communicative basis. However, the meeting of the proverb in the speech of the hero of the work, and the fact that the hero is a representative of the common people, indicates that the proverb is used for the purpose of individualizing the speech. After all, it is natural for representatives of ordinary people to change and use folk proverbs in their speech. It can be understood that the quoted proverb was created as an analogy to the proverb, *" Be a king in another country, be a gado in your own country ."* Based on the observation and analysis of the writer's activities in the life process of the people, the proverb is given in a modified form through the speech of the hero, which is also an example of skill in using language tools. After all, proverbs are considered as a means of vividly embodying the thoughts that the creator wants to express in artistic texts.

Talented writers, in addition to using folk proverbs, create proverbs that correspond to folk proverbs in content and form and direct the writer's idea towards disclosure. For example, if there is a blind devil, the writer, using a *famous proverb of your sect* , puts forward the idea that *if the work is carried out under the guidance of a cunning and flawed person, it will lead to the wrong path* . At the same time, such proverbs also indicate the speaker's subjective assessment of the person against whom they are used. *The Goza expert is now so powerful that if there is a coup d'état in Africa, the first thing to ask is whether Aleksandr Shaymardonovich had a hand in it. If your friend is a devil, your religion is known* ("Lolazor"). The proverb has a deep logical basis in its content, and it is related to a person who, through his cunning, passes his word to the leader and commits bad deeds. One of the proverbs created on the basis of such logical considerations was used by the writer as an example to those *who follow* the path of living contentedly, enjoying the fruits of their labor, and enjoying without *labor* . *All time is not the same time, brother Elomonov! The one who doesn't find it gets kicked in the teeth, and the one who eats gets kicked in the tooth without finding it.* "Resignation") is a proverb. The writer quotes this proverb as an example to people who want to live to the fullest without doing unsatisfying work, and expresses his attitude towards such people based on the content of the proverb. Or expressed through the character's inner speech. (*Raim Gaybarov was right -someone's mind is not smart, it's hard if you can't separate black and white.* The proverb "Resignation") is used to express the writer's idea about the consequences of acting on the instructions of others without thinking. Proverbs of a comparative nature also perform the function of evaluation. It often expresses the attitude of the speaker to the listener. For example, - *said Elomonov with a sweet pain in his body, - would the dead come back to life, Buyukjon! - A dead camel is a living mouse!* "Resignation". This proverb, expressed through the speech of the character of the work, also expresses the attitude towards the interlocutor. In it, the writer tries to justify his idea on the basis of the antinomy of experienced-inexperienced, big-small by comparing a person with a lot of experience to a person without experience. <u>There is no shame in the term </u>applied to a writer's individual style (*Ms. Muhsina's gold ring was a lot of gold bracelets, but there is no shame in saying it is necessary. Yakhasboev brought one more gold ring.* "Lolazor") proverb is also characteristic. This proverb means that the bettor <u>can make any bet .</u> In this respect, the condition of the hero of the work is also appropriate, because of this, it is fulfilled. By using proverbs in his work, the writer assumes that any situation can arise in life, in the course of human relations, and that in such cases, ideas with a deep meaning expressed in folk proverbs can help a person to behave in the right way.

It seems that folk proverbs in artistic texts are not only linguistic tools that provide artistic impact and have aesthetic value, but also are an example of morals that should be mastered by the reader as an important part of artistic text. Writers also use proverbs in order to ensure that the reader draws conclusions from the proverb and makes changes in his life based on these conclusions. This shows that proverbs are multifunctional in the composition of literary texts.

CONCLUSION

The issue of the skillful use of language tools in a literary text is an important process in the analysis of a literary text, and it is the basis for studying the language of a literary work in world linguistics. Therefore, the study and analysis of the appropriate use of language tools in a work of art is a general philological issue, because fiction is important for the development of the literary language, as it is the main tool that determines the development of the literary language. is a manifest source. The artist is judged based on his work. Every creator reflects life artistically by his deep thinking, artistically describing things in life that others have not developed, awakens aesthetic feelings in people, creates artistic paints, images, allusions using various features of vocabulary tools.

Murad Muhammad Dost is a writer who is distinguished by his sensitivity to language tools, and in his works he skillfully uses the rich possibilities of the vernacular, especially the tools of simple colloquial forms of the language. The language of the writer's works is silent, devoid of descriptions, but they attract the reader based on the uniqueness of the expression process, the simplicity and attractiveness of the narrative. In the works of the writer, there is a style of embodiment of thought in the imagination of the speaker, which is hardly found in other creators. This style of expression and the proper use of all the tools available in the common language ensured that a unique attractive and juicy language appeared in the writer's works.

The linguopoetic analysis of the works of the writer Murad Muhammad Dost led to the following conclusions.

1. Although there are many scientific studies devoted to the analysis of the language of artistic works in Uzbek linguistics, the existing studies devoted to the study of the language of Uzbek fiction literature, which has a long history, skillful creators and mature works, cannot be considered sufficient. There are enough creators and works of art in Uzbek literature that need to be studied linguistically.

2. The textual structure of Murad Muhammad Dost's works was the basis for the selection of language tools. In the writer's works, the author's and character's speech is mixed, the events that happened through the character's speech are expressed in the way of thinking about things in the imagination, it shows the writer's unique style of expression.

3. Murad Mohammad Dost is a unique creator in choosing words and using them in speech. First of all, he chooses words that correspond to the essence of the thought to be expressed, express the meaning in a clear and understandable way, are distinguished by the features of artistic coloring, and use them in accordance with the essence of the speech.

4. The works of Murad Muhammad Dost cover a rich lexical content. It should be recognized that common words are

important vocabulary units in the writer's works in terms of the use of oral speech tools. The writer used not only the meanings and methodological possibilities of these lexical tools, but also took into account their folk signs. As a result, through these tools, the language of the writer's works was brought closer to the vernacular, the comprehensibility and simplicity of the work was organized.

5. The main feature that characterizes the writer's works from the point of view of language is that they are formed on the basis of lexical tools characteristic of ordinary speech.

6. Synonyms are an important factor in determining the artistic-aesthetic value of a literary text. Expression of different levels of meaning in synonyms, emotional coloring in word meaning is a wide opportunity for the writer. Murad Muhammad Dost is a creator who skillfully used this opportunity. Especially in the work of the writer, finding and using the synonyms of the word in the literary language in oral speech fulfilled the tasks of ensuring the nationalism of the work and characterizing the speech of the characters. Synonyms were able to show their brilliance in the writer's works. Synonyms are also used in order to give artistic color, enthusiasm, and decoration to the artistic text through the expression of the meaning in different colors.

7. Literary language is interpreted as a language created by word artists, which implies the contribution of creators to the

development of language. Murad Mohammad Dost's work is also characteristic in this respect. In addition to activating existing lexical tools in his works, he also created new words based on the word formation patterns of the language.

8. Among the lexical units actively used in the works of Murad Muhammad Dost, idioms can be singled out. Idioms are a complex language unit in terms of structure, unconventionality, the connection of the meaning of the lexical tools with the new meaning expressed by the idiom. Most of the idioms in Murad Muhammad Dost's works are of an occasional nature and are characteristic of the writer's individual style.

9. Folk proverbs are important lexical tools in a work of art, and they are used for various purposes, including as a means of demonstration. Writer Murad Muhammad Dost's works are also decorated with folk proverbs. According to the use of proverbs found in the writer's works, they form groups such as proverbs in folk version, modified version, and proverbs specific to the writer's individual style.

10. Murad Muhammad Dost's works are linguistically rich, observing that all vocabulary tools available in the national language are used to create certain methodological possibilities, which shows that the writer has a unique individuality in the use of language.

REFERENCES
NORMATIVE LEGAL DOCUMENTS AND PUBLICATIONS OF METHODOLOGICAL SIGNIFICANCE

1. Mirziyoev Sh. Resolutely continuing our path of national development, we will rise to a new level! - Tashkent: Uzbekistan, 2017. - 592 p.

2. Mirziyoev Sh. The approval of our people is the highest evaluation given to our activities. - Tashkent: Uzbekistan, 2018. - 507 p.

3. Mirziyoev Sh. We will build our great future together with our brave and noble people. - Tashkent: Uzbekistan, 2017. - 486 p.

MONOGRAPH, STUDY GUIDE, SCIENTIFIC ARTICLES, SCIENTIFIC COLLECTIONS

4. Abdurakhmanov G'. About learning the language of a literary work // Issues of the methodology of teaching the Uzbek language. - Tashkent: Science, 1966. - B. 4-12.

5. Abdurakhmanov G'. About the literary style of the contemporary Uzbek language // Uzbek language and literature. Tashkent, 1992. - No. 5-6.

6. Atullah Hosseini. Badoyi'-us-sanoyi'. - Tashkent: Literature and art named after G'. Ghulam, 1981. - 398 p.

7. Akhmanova O.S. Dictionary of linguistic terms. - M.: Soviet encyclopedia, 1966. - 606 c .

8. Bally Sh. French style. – M.: Foreign Literature. 1961. -S. 344.

9. Bakirov P.U. Semantics and structure of nominacentric proverbs. – Tashkent: Fan, 2006. – B. 297.Begmatov E. Lexical layers of the current Uzbek literary language. - Tashkent: Science, 1985. - 200 p.

8. Vasileva A.N. Khudojestvennaya rech. - M.: Russky Yazyk, 1983. - 255 p.

9. Vinogradov V.V. O language of godly literature. - M.: izdatelsva, 1959. 360 p.

10. Grigorev V.P. Poetics is a word. - M.: Nauka, 1979. - 343 p.

11. Daniyorov Kh. Some issues of learning the language of works of art // Issues of Uzbek linguistics. - Samarkand, 1943.

12. Daniyorov H., Samadov Q. Hamid Olimjon's innovation in the use of language // Eastern star, 1959. - #1.

13. Efimov A.I. Stylistics of artistic speech. – M.: Enlightenment, 1961. – 519 p.Joraeva B. Linguistic foundations of the formation of Uzbek folk proverbs. - Tashkent: Akademnashr, 2019. - B. 224.

13. Imamova G. Nationalism and artistic speech. - Tashkent: 2004 - 28 pages.

14. Yoldoshev B. Stylistics of artistic speech. - Samarkand, 1982.

15. Yoldoshev M. Secrets of the word shepherd. - Tashkent: Spirituality. 2002. - 79 p.

16. Kalinin A.V. Lexicon of the Russian language. - M.: Moscow University, 1978. - S. 231.

17. Karimov S. Artistic style of the Uzbek language. - Samarkand: 1992. - 139 p.

18. Mahkamov N. Ermatov I. Explanatory dictionary of linguistic terms. - Tashkent: Science, 2013. - P.143.

19. Mahmudov N. About the linguopoetics of Abdulla Qahhor's stories // Uzbek language and literature. 1987. No. 4. - B. 34-38

20. Mahmudov N. Linguistics of similes in Oybek's poetry // Uzbek language and literature. - Tashkent, 1985. - #6. - B. 48-50.

21. Makhmaraimova Sh. Linguistic culture. - Tashkent: Publishing house named after Cholpon, 2017. - 163 p.

22. Mirzaev M., Usmanov S., Rasulov I. Uzbek language. - Tashkent: Teacher, 1970. - 266 p.

23. Normurodov R. Artistic skills of Shukur Kholmirzaev. - Tashkent: Writers' Union of Uzbekistan Literary Foundation, 2003. - B. 103.

24. Sabirdinov A. Word and image in Oybek's poetry. - Tashkent: Akademnashr, 2010. - 87 p.

25. Q. Samadov Oybek is an artist of words. - Tashkent: 1965.

26. Q. Samadov Aibek's language skills. - Tashkent: 1965.

27. Q. Samadov Methodology of the Uzbek language. - Tashkent: Teacher, 1991. - 51 p.

28. Solijonov Y. Speech and style. - Tashkent: Cholpon, 2002. - 127 p.

29. Tursunov U., Mukhtorov J., Rahmatullaev Sh. Modern Uzbek literary language. - Tashkent: Teacher, 1975. - 258 p.

30. Toraev D. Time and creative responsibility. - Tashkent: New generation, 2004. - 129 p.

31. Umurkulov B. Lexicon of poetic speech. - Tashkent: Science, 1990. - 109 p.

32. Umurkulov B. Word in fiction. - Tashkent: Science, 1993. - 131 p.

33. Shmelev D.N. Slova i obraz. - M.: Nauka, 1964. - S. 38.

34. Shoabdurahmanov Sh. The language and style of Oibek's novel // Eastern Star, 1965.

35. Shomaksudov Sh., Shorahmedov Sh. Wisdom. Explanatory dictionary of Uzbek proverbs. - Tashkent: 1990. - B. 8.

36. Shukurov N. On G. Gulom's skill in using the language // Problems of the Uzbek language and literature, 1959. - #4.

37. Orinboev B. Problems of Uzbek language colloquial speech syntax. - Tashkent: Science, 1974. - 148 p.

38. Kuronov D. Poetics of shepherd's prose. - Tashkent: Sharq, 2004. - 287 p.

39. Kuronov D. Theoretical notes. - Tashkent: Akademnashr, 2018. - 125 p.

40. Kochkortoev I. Stylistics of artistic speech. - Tashkent: Teacher, 1976. - 86 p.

41. Kochkortoev I. Lexical synonyms and their main types // Uzbek language and literature. 1984, No. 4. - B. 4-7.

DISSERTATIONS AND ABSTRACTS

42. Andaniyazova D. Lingupoetics of onamastic units in literary text. Doctor of Philosophy in Philology (PhD) ... diss. autoref. - Tashkent, 2017.

43. Babaeva S. Lexical and stylistic features of Hamid Alimdzhan's poetry: author. diss... cand. philol. Sciences. - Tashkent, 1989. - 17 p.Babadjanov F. Linguistic features of modern Uzbek dramas (based on Behbudi and Avloni dramas): philol. science. nomz... diss. autoref. - Samarkand, 2002. - 23 p.

43. Bafoev B. Lexik produced by Alishera Navoi (lexical-semantic, statistical and tematic research). Diss .. . Dr. Philol. science - Tashkent, 1989.

44. Boymirzaeva S. Linguistic study of Oybek's prose: philology. science. nomz... diss. autoref. - Samarkand, 2004. - 23 p.

45. Jumanazarova G.U. Lexical and linguopoetic features of the epic "Shirin bilan Shakar". filol.fan.nom. ... diss. - Tashkent: 2008.

46. Jumanazarova G. Linguistics of the language of Fazil Yoldosh's epics. Philol. science. dr. ... diss. autoref. - T.: 2017.

47. Ibragimov A. Linguistic, semantic and genetic study of the lexicon of Babur's works. Philol. science. dr. ... diss. autoref. - Tashkent, 2008 .

48. Y'oldoshev M. Linguistics of literary text. Philol. science. dr. ... diss. autoref. - Tashkent, 2008. - 48 p.

49. Karimov S. Yazyk i stil produced by Zulfii: autoref. diss... cand. Philol. science - Tashkent, 1982. - 16 s.

50. Karimov S. Artistic style of the Uzbek language. Autoref. diss... Ph.D. Philol. science - Tashkent: 1993.

51. Kilichev E. Archaism and history in prose Sadriddina Aini: autoref. diss... cand. Philol. science – Tashkent, 1969. - 30 s.

52. Kilichev E. Archaisms and historicisms in the prose of Sadriddin Aini: author. diss... cand. philol. Sciences. - Tashkent, 1969. - 30 p.

53. Kuchkartaev I. Phraseological innovation of A. Kahkhara. Abstract diss ... cand. philol. Sciences. - Tashkent, 1965.

54. Mirzaev I. Problems of linguistic and poetic interpretation of the poetic text. Abstract diss... doc. philol. Sciences. - Tashkent, 1992..

52. Rahimov A. Poetics of the Uzbek novel. Autoref. diss... Ph.D. Philol. science - Tashkent: 1993.

53. Sayidov Yo. Lexicon of Fitrat's artistic works: Philology. science. name ... diss. autoref. - Tashkent, 2001. - 24 p.

54. Solijonov Y. Poetics of artistic speech in Uzbek prose of the 80s-90s of the 20th century: Filol. science. name ... diss. autoref. - Tashkent: TAI. 2003. - 52 p.

55. Turdialiev B. Khamza i Uzbek literary language of the 20th century: Autoref. dis s ... d-ra filol. science - Tashkent, 1988.

56. Turdialieva D. Linguistic features of Uzbek folk proverbs: Philology. Ph.D. in philosophy. ... diss. autoref. – Against, 2019

57. Kholmonova Z. Study of the "Boburnoma" lexicon: Doctor of Philology ... diss. autoref. - Tashkent, 2009. - 51 p.

58. Khudoyberganova D. Semantic and stylistic idiosyncrasies of constructional similarity in the Uzbek language: diss... kand. Philol. science - Tashkent, 1989. - 119 p.

59. Shoabdurahmanov Sh. Lexicon of "Ravshan" epic: Autoref. diss... cand. Philol. science - Tashkent: TAI. 1949. - 22 p.

60. Shodieva D. Lingupoetics of Muhammad Yusuf's poetry: Philol.fan. name ... diss. autoref. - Tashkent, 2007

61. Shodmonova D. Linguistic features of Abdulla Oripov's poetry: Philol. Ph.D. in philosophy. ... diss. autoref. - Karshi, 2019. - 52 p.

62. Yariev B. Language poetry Maksuda Sheykhzade: autoref. diss... cand. Philol. science - Tashkent, 1979. - 22 p.

63. Yakubbekova M. Linguistic features of Uzbek folk songs: Phil. science. dr. ... diss. - Tashkent, 2005. - 237 p.

64. Yuldashev B. Yazyk i stil proizvedeniy Saida Akhmada: Autoref. diss... cand. Philol. science - Tashkent, 1979. - 16 p.

65. Kasimova M.B. Linguistic characteristics of the individuality of artistic speech (based on the works of Uncle Murad): Filol.fan.nomz. ...diss.authorref. - T., 2007. - 23 p.

66. Kilichev E. Archaism and history in prose Sadriddin Ayny. Autoref. dis s .. sugar Philol. science - Tashkent, 1973.

Dictionaries

67. Rahmatullaev Sh. An explanatory phraseological dictionary of the Uzbek language. - T.: Teacher, 1978

68. An explanatory dictionary of the Uzbek language. 5 volumes.- Tashkent: "National Encyclopedia of Uzbekistan" State Scientific Publishing House, 2006. // www.ziyouz.com library

69. Linguistic encyclopedic dictionary. - M., 1986.

70. Hojiev A. An explanatory dictionary of synonyms of the Uzbek language. - T.: "Teacher", 1974.

Fiction

71. Murad Muhammad Dost. "Galatepaga qaytish yoxud saodatman G'aybarov rivoyati". -Tashkent: Gafur Gulam, 2009.

72. Murad Muhammad Dost. "Iste'fo". -Tashkent, 1989.

73. Murad Muhammad Dost. "Mustafo". -Tashkent, 1989.

74. Murad Muhammad Dost. "Lolazor". -Tashkent: Uzbekistan, 2016.

Internet educational resources

75. http:// www.ziyouz.com library. Gulkhani "Zarbolmasal". -Tashkent: Teacher, 1972.

76. The speech of the President of the Republic of Uzbekistan Shavkat Mirziyoev during his visit to "Alley of Writers" . http: // www. newspaper . en . May 20, 2020.

www.ingramcontent.com/pod-product-compliance
Lightning Source LLC
LaVergne TN
LVHW021237080526
838199LV00088B/4555